Looking into the Well

Supervision of Spiritual Directors

Maureen Conroy, R.S.M.

Foreword by George Aschenbrenner, S.J.

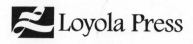

Loyola Press

Chicago

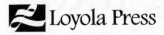
Loyola Press

3441 North Ashland Avenue
Chicago, Illinois 60657

All Scriptural quotations are from the New American Bible
(New York: Thomas Nelson, 1971)
Cover illustration by William Gorman
Electronic artwork on p. 162 by Meg Elliott Smith

Cover and Interior design by Nancy Gruenke

Library of Congress Cataloging-in-Publication Data
Conroy, Maureen
Looking into the Well: Supervision of Spiritual Directors/
Maureen Conroy
       p.   cm.
  Includes bibliographical references and index.
  ISBN 0-8294-0827-4
  1. Spiritual directors—Supervision of. 2. Spiritual direction—Study
and teaching. I. Title
BX2350.7.C675 1995
253.5'3—dc20   94-43267
                                             CIP

Printed in the United States of America
98 99 00 01 02 / 10 9 8 7 6 5 4 3

Dedication

I dedicate this book to the many people I have journeyed with as supervisor, teacher, and mentor in the spiritual direction training programs at the Upper Room Spiritual Center and in the graduate programs in spirituality at Creighton University, Omaha, Nebraska; and Chestnut Hill College, Chestnut Hill, Pennsylvania. My experience with these dedicated individuals who deeply love the ministry of spiritual direction has been both an inspiration and a profound learning experience for me. I have learned with them as well as shared my knowledge and experience. I will always be grateful to these "companions on the journey" for what they have taught me. I hold each of them in my heart and prayer.

Jesus and the Woman at the Well

Jesus, tired from the journey, sat down at the well. When a Samaritan woman came to draw water, Jesus said to her: "Give me a drink." The woman said to him, "You are a Jew. How can you ask me, a Samaritan and a woman, for a drink?" Jesus replied:

"If only you recognized God's gift, and who it is that is asking you for a drink, you would have asked him instead, and he would have given you living water."

"Sir," she challenged him, "you do not have a bucket and this well is deep. Where do you expect to get this flowing water?" Jesus replied:

"Everyone who drinks this water will be thirsty again. But whoever drinks the water I give will never be thirsty; no, the water I give shall become a fountain within, leaping up to provide eternal life."

The woman said to him, "Give me this water, sir, so that I shall not grow thirsty and have to keep coming here to draw water" (Jn 4:6–15).

Contents

Foreword

Chilling violence and a deeply embedded individualism plague parts of our world. Their expression can, at times, be so dramatic and obvious as to distract us from something else that is also happening in our midst. A growing spiritual hunger is gnawing away at the human heart, stretching its desire from discontent to the lengths of God. Though not of dizzying proportions, this hunger of spirit is real and revealed in a great variety of evidence and within many people. Not limited to one class of people nor to one geographical place, the hunger ranges far and wide: rich and poor, lay and religious, women and men, east, west, north, and south.

Frightened and deeply confused, people are searching for love and meaning. Increasingly their search is turning to the possibility of a God whose faithful love is promised and revealed in Jesus. How to relate to this Jesus? How to discover hidden meaning in such a relationship? No one experience will suffice. Parishes, spiritual centers, retreat houses, and other pastoral centers are creating a variety of experiences and programs to help people both to answer these questions and to assuage their growing spiritual hunger.

As the director of the Jesuit Center for Spiritual Growth in Wernersville, Pennsylvania, I watch this phenomena with intense interest and some skepticism. Such a diversified variety of programs—from a thirty-day experience of the *Spiritual*

Exercises to a weekend of Enneagram spirituality to three days of directed prayer to a single day for health-care professionals—can be both blessing and curse. Sometimes the more diversified the programs, the more superficial and vague the experience. No one is sure what happened, or what was supposed to happen. As a result, nothing of much import occurs.

The situation today is clearly calling for ingenuity to which we must hearken. Something profound and professional must inspire this modern multiplicity of spiritual programs. We must rigorously appreciate and carefully reverence the dynamics at work whenever God's loving Spirit instigates human response. These dynamics involve a unique and awesome beauty. Thus they always form an essential part of the development of any mature love relationship with Jesus.

Such love, if it is to be significant in any profound, dependable, and promising way for the future, will always be forged of the spontaneous, impulsive movements and countermovements of our daily consciousness. Finally, this love of Jesus will take shape in a personal faith relationship that will gradually assimilate and integrate more and more of our person in response to God's infinite loving invitation.

It is precisely regarding this crucial personal faith relationship that Maureen Conroy's book makes a very valuable contribution. *Looking into the Well* is the first book-length treatment of supervision for spiritual directors. It continues the theories developed in *The Discerning Heart* (Loyola University Press, 1993). In that book Maureen traced the dynamics involved in the discovery and development of a relationship with a personal loving God. Using the examples of Ignatius of Loyola and various modern case studies, she showed how the Rules for Discernment in the *Spiritual Exercises* help us make sense of our human consciousness in order to form a dependable relationship with God. It also provided guidance for spiritual directors in their effort to help directees develop a more personal and profound relationship with God.

Looking into the Well describes the experience and process of supervision for spiritual directors. Surely not everyone is meant to be a spiritual director, nor is everyone meant to be a supervisor. But without the professional supervision that spiritual directors deserve, the variety of programs available would be less competent and less trustworthy. Supervision, just as spiritual direction itself, is meant to have a trickle-down effect and thus serves a valuable enriching purpose. As director of a spiritual center, I am aware of the important role supervision plays as a great variety of direction-experiences are tailored to the spiritual need and hunger of our diversified clientele. Professional supervision, whether in a peer group or one-on-one setting, can provide a foundational center and offer stability among the burgeoning variety of spiritual experiences in today's church.

Looking into the Well is clear, practical, and, always, experiential. By emphasizing the director's inner spiritual experience with the directee, the author distinguishes supervision from counseling and consultation, although, supervision can occasionally overlap with these two processes. Maureen Conroy has many years of experience in direction and supervision. That wealth of background keeps the book helpfully experiential. Although reading about supervision is not the same surely as actually receiving of supervision, *Looking into the Well* comes awfully close. My practice of direction and supervision cannot be the same after reading *Looking into the Well.* Throughout the book I felt as though I were being supervised.

Buried deep within every human heart is the restless yearning for contemplative intimacy with a dearly loving God in Jesus. Augustine reminded us of this yearning in the opening of his *Confessions.* But our own experience is also an insistent reminder of this truth. Such divine intimacy is not something that is so extraordinary and abstruse as to be unavailable to every believer, indeed, to every human being. Granting the reality of a loving God so attractively revealed in Jesus, we discover a daily invitation to unitive living with this Jesus in the variety of our inner experiences. Admittedly such variety can be so confusing at times as to cry out for interpretation in faith. For this reason, *Looking into the Well* forcefully describes supervision as evocative, contemplative, and discerning. Rather than simply telling the supervisor what to do, Maureen displays her own evocative and contemplative style as she provides the necessary interpretation of discernment by spotlighting in all of our inner experience the inspiring presence of God.

The care and competence of the book's style reveals the author's great desire to inspire supervisors and directors. Supervision is presented not as a threatening or intimidating experience but rather as an enriching and attractive one. It is described as a shared experience of encouragement and support among servant directors helping one another to be more responsive to a God who is eager to continue the transformation of our universe.

What *Looking into the Well* envisions is of no less proportion. Supervision (and spiritual direction) is always much more than a simple one-to-one faith-sharing. The book's implications and context make it clear that supervision ultimately hopes for a whole new creation throughout the universe, as promised in the beauty of Jesus. This new creation is precisely what the Samaritan woman in John 4 found reflected in the well of Jesus' eyes. Maureen Conroy has peered into those eyes. *Looking into the Well* mirrors the infinitely expansive heart of Jesus and challenges the sensitive work of many supervisors and directors.

George Aschenbrenner, S.J.
Jesuit Center for Spiritual Growth
Wernersville, Pennsylvania

Introduction

Spiritual direction helps people grow in a personal relationship with God and assists them to discover God's presence in their life. A growing reality in the ministry of spiritual direction is the importance of supervision. Since 1982 I have had the privilege of supervising spiritual directors in two training programs at the Upper Room Spiritual Center in Neptune, New Jersey. I have conducted workshops on supervision for spiritual center and retreat staffs with training programs. During the summers since 1986 I have taught the two practicum courses in spiritual direction in the Christian Spirituality Program at Creighton University, Omaha, Nebraska. Many experienced spiritual directors who supervise students between prepracticum and postpracticum have expressed a strong desire to learn more about supervision. I myself have received a great deal of supervision during two training programs and during ongoing peer group supervision.

Many developmental programs for spiritual directors are evolving throughout the world. While working on the committee that plans an annual national symposium for centers, retreat houses, colleges, and universities that have programs for spiritual directors, I have connected with more than one hundred programs in the United States. Training program coordinators are realizing the need for a common understanding of the supervisory purposes, content, process, and skills required to help directors-in-training develop their knowledge of and skills for spiritual direction.

As a result of these many enriching experiences, I am convinced of the essential need for supervision in order to become a skilled and discerning spiritual director. Both individuals and groups are realizing the importance of supervision as a way to develop the skills of spiritual direction.

Looking into the Well is intended to assist the development of a common understanding of supervision for spiritual directors. Although similarities in the approaches and processes to supervision among counselors, pastoral counselors, spiritual directors, and clinical pastoral educators can be found, differences also exist. Supervision of spiritual directors is unique because it contains a contemplative component and focuses on discerning interior movements. These two crucial differences undergird all aspects of supervision—its purpose, its content, its process, and its skills.

This book is for spiritual directors, supervisors, and educators of spiritual directors. It serves several functions. First, it is intended to be an experiential aid for spiritual directors to reflect on their ministry of spiritual direction and their experience of supervision and, most important, to help them develop an ongoing posture of self-supervision and a discerning vision of heart. Second, it can help experienced supervisors ponder their experience of conducting individual and peer group supervision, sharpen their supervision skills, and develop a discerning heart. Third, it can be used as an educational manual for experienced spiritual directors who are beginning to supervise other spiritual directors and who want to learn the purposes, process, and skills of supervision. Fourth, it can serve as a handbook for those who are developing and conducting educational programs and who want to reflect on the experience of and approach to supervision in their programs.

Looking into the Well is divided into two parts. Part I articulates the assumptions and purposes of spiritual direction and supervision, describing its content and the process involved, exploring its skills, and offering three case studies by way of illustration. It describes two models for peer group supervision and contains an actual peer group session. Further it explains seven phases in the supervision experience that help spiritual directors' growth in discernment, and it articulates key dynamics to assist supervisors' development of a discerning heart. Finally, it discusses how supervision is a significant learning experience and explains the difference between supervision and consultation. By giving many examples throughout, the book strives to integrate theory and practice. Each chapter concludes with questions for reflection and discussion for both supervisors and spiritual directors and offers an invitation for everyone to participate in a contemplative moment and a prayer.

To describe clearly the supervision experience and process an analogy is made comparing the supervision of spiritual directors to the story of Jesus with the woman at the well. The supervisor, Jesus, and the spiritual director, with reverence and care, "look into the well" of the spiritual director's interior directing space. Each chapter describes aspects of this analogy. The conclusion of Part I contains a diagram of a well that illustrates the various dimensions of supervision. It also includes a spiritual director's prayer and a supervisor's prayer. Moreover references are made to interior movements within spiritual directors and the importance of directors' attending to their own interior life. This focus on interior movements is rooted in the Rules for Discernment in the *Spiritual Exercises* of Ignatius of Loyola. Although the focus is inherent in all approaches to spirituality, Ignatius was one of the few people to link the development of the interior life and our experience of God with spiritual consolation and spiritual desolation. *Looking into the Well* experientially applies Ignatius's descriptions of interior movements to a spiritual director's direction experience and interior development.

Part II presents a number of learning experiences for spiritual directors, supervisors, and training teams that can be used for personal reflection as well as for group discussion and role-playing. These learning experiences include prayer experiences, summaries of situational types to bring to supervision, case studies, evaluation instruments for spiritual directors and supervisors, and other reflection tools.

The appendixes will be of particular interest to educators of spiritual directors who are beginning a program or those who have already done so and who want to reflect on its various components.

Supervision of spiritual directors is both an art and a science. It is an art in that it requires a constant attentiveness to the spiritual director's interior space and to God's lively presence. Each supervision session is different because each supervisor and spiritual director brings to it his or her own unique self and experience. It is a science because it involves a disciplined focus, a clear process, and specific skills. Part of the challenge of being a good supervisor is integrating both the art and science of supervision into a unified reality and a congruent approach.

Supervision is at the heart of learning to be a spiritual director. It is the way to apply theoretical knowledge about spiritual direction and the spiritual life to experiential learning. It is the means to transform general awarenesses about spiritual direction and discernment into concrete knowledge. Indeed, supervision is the key to unlocking the treasure of experiential learnings that are necessary to be a spiritual director; it is, in short, an essential way to develop a contemplative and discerning heart for the ministry of spiritual direction.

Whether you are a spiritual director or a supervisor, I invite you to stay in touch with your own experience as you read these chapters so that a deeper experiential understanding of spiritual direction and supervision can unfold within your mind and heart.

A Note on Terminology

Within the helping profession, programs for the development of spiritual directors are referred to in various ways, including "training programs," "mentoring programs," "educational programs," and "developmental programs." These terms will be used interchangeably throughout the book.

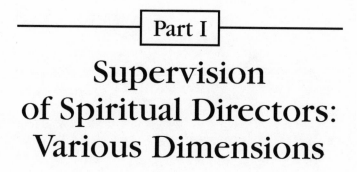

Part I

Supervision of Spiritual Directors: Various Dimensions

1

Self-Awareness
and Interior Freedom:
Assumptions and Purposes
in the Supervision
of Spiritual Directors

Spiritual directors are companions with others on their journey to God. As companions, they share in others' struggles and joys. They are not detached bystanders. Rather they actively help others to develop a relationship with God. Spiritual directors serve as a resting place for those who want to savor God's loving presence and explore God's seeming absence. They become a contemplative presence for those who want to discover how God has been moving in their hearts and how God has been active in their lives. Because spiritual directors are intimately involved with others' life and religious experience, they need others to accompany them as they help and support their directees. Since they experience various interior movements while directing, they need the caring presence of another person to explore these movements. This chapter (1) discusses the assumptions undergirding spiritual direction and supervision; (2) examines the purposes of spiritual direction and supervision; (3) explores the experience of interior movements during direction sessions; and (4) and clarifies the supervisory function.

Assumptions in Spiritual Direction and Supervision

Certain assumptions permeate both spiritual direction and supervision, such as the belief that God is present in all human experience. Through personal prayer and spiritual direction God's *implicit* presence becomes *explicit* in peoples' experience. God is a self-communicating God who reveals self through creation, Scripture, life experience, human relationships, solitude, and prayer. God's self-giving is eternal and can occur in a moment of time. God's transcendent presence becomes immanent in human experience, and, by staying alert, individuals can in turn become aware of God's immanent presence. God communicates self not only in universal ways but also in personal ways through individual experiences, personalities, desires, and needs. In other words, God can be experienced in hearts, minds, imaginations, psyches, and bodies.

As individuals experience God's self-communication interiorly, they come to *know* God, not only know *about* God. They experience spontaneous interior reactions, some of which correspond to God's ways and others that do not. God longs for response but ultimately grants humanity with free will. Personal brokenness, sinfulness, blindness, and life struggles can prevent individuals from responding to God's self-communication. But these challenges can also open them to God's desire to redeem, heal, and make whole.

Several important assumptions about spiritual directors affect the spiritual direction and supervision process. Spiritual directors are human beings, and as human beings they are both gifted and broken, interiorly free and unfree, accepting feelings and denying feelings. They are affected by their own and their directees' resistance. Spiritual directors' unresolved issues, such as denied or repressed feelings, can prevent them from helping directees to look deeply at their life circumstances and savor fully their religious experience. Directors' ability to notice their own vulnerable areas and feel their own feelings affects their ability to help directees explore their experiences in-depth. As they continue to acknowledge their own resistance and examine their own vulnerable areas, directors can grow interiorly free and, subsequently, empathize with directees' experiences.

For all of these reasons, spiritual directors require supervision. They need time, experience, and assistance in order to grow more aware of how their giftedness and brokenness manifest themselves in their ministry.

Spiritual directors are individuals who are in relationship with God and have a deep desire to help others grow in relationship with God. On their spiritual journey, they need to develop a capacity to be attentive to and linger with their own experiences of God. Their ability to help others do so is affected by how they linger with their own experiences. As spiritual directors learn these skills, they grow more keenly aware of other people's interior movements—both obvious and subtle—toward and away from God.

Therefore, spiritual direction and supervision are God-centered, trinitarian experiences in various ways. First, the directee, spiritual director, and supervisor are each in relationship with God as the Trinity of Creator, Redeemer, and Life-giving Spirit. That is, they each have their own vital and growing relationship with God. Second, the spiritual direction experience is the threefold communion of the spiritual director, directee, and God in a heartfelt connection with one another. Third, supervision is a triadic encounter of the spiritual director, supervisor, and God working together for the spiritual director's growth. "Where two or three are gathered in my name, there am I in the midst of them" (Mt 18:20). Awareness of God's presence in spiritual direction and supervision sessions is essential, resulting in spiritual directors becoming interiorly freer to linger more deeply with directees' experiences.

Purposes and Skills of Spiritual Direction

To understand the purposes of supervision, spiritual directors and supervisors need to remember the purposes of spiritual direction. The primary goal of spiritual direction is to help individuals *grow in a personal relationship with God*. Specific purposes are to assist people to

- recognize, pay attention to, and respond to God's specific self-communication in life, prayer, and relationships;

- savor, relive, and enjoy the affective touches of God;

- notice differences that take place because of their affective experiences of God;

- explore God's seeming absence;

- recognize, explore, and uncover areas of resistance, darkness, and unfreedom that prevent an individual response to God's presence;

- sift through interior movements;

- grow in deeper intimacy with God; and

- experience greater interior freedom, deeper joy, more grace-filled decisions, a more integrated life, and healthier relationships with self, others, and the world.

For these purposes to be realized, spiritual directors must develop a variety of contemplative and discernment skills that are not only verbal techniques but also inner stances of the heart and spirit. In essence these skills function as basic principles that are grounded in the interior life of directees, the spiritual focus of spiritual directors, and the presence of God. The contemplative skills spiritual directors need to develop include the ability to

- listen in a nonjudgmental and accepting way;

- be aware of God's presence during direction sessions and grow in the experiential knowledge that spiritual direction is a Trinitarian experience;

- develop a reverent attitude and an evocative approach so that directees can notice, savor, and relive particular experiences of God;

- help people pray in a personal, affective, and relational way; and

- give concrete suggestions for prayer based on the experience shared.

Spiritual directors also must develop discernment skills, that is, the ability to sift through *interior movements*. As people grow in a personal relationship with God, they experience interior movements toward and away from God, and they talk about these movements in spiritual direction. For instance, as a directee notices and savors God's embrace, he or she may experience *consolation* or *movement toward God*—peace and joy in God's embrace or a deep gratitude. On the contrary, as a directee lingers with God's embrace, he or she may experience *desolation* or *countermovement*—fear of intimacy with God or feelings of unworthiness that take the form of avoidance of prayer or distractions in prayer. Therefore, directors must help individuals to

- be attentive to movements toward and away from God;

- savor and respond to those movements that are helping growth in union with God; and

- explore, unpack, and become freer of countermovements.

Thus the purposes and skills of spiritual direction are rooted in contemplation and discernment.

Contemplation means noticing, absorbing, and savoring God's self-communication. Discernment involves exploring individuals' interior movements as they respond to God's self-revelation.

Spiritual Directors' Experience of Interior Movements

While spiritual directors are companioning others, they also experience a variety of interior reactions, such as *consolation* or *movement toward God*, in that they are drawn into the directee's experience—attracted, engaged, and resonating with the sharing of that experience. They may have a lively sense of God's presence and experience union with the directee and God. They may experience spiritual joy, gratitude, peace, love, and new life (sometimes these fruits of the Spirit are accompanied by tears). They are aware of the guiding presence of the Spirit of God and allow God to lead them.

They may experience empathy and compassion for their directees, feeling a sense of God's love for them.

Spiritual directors experience consolation because they are prayerful people themselves, drinking regularly from the living waters of God's loving presence. They strive to be attentive to God's presence in their own life and during direction sessions. The more they companion others on their spiritual journey, the more deeply they grow in awareness that spiritual direction is a trinitarian encounter—God, the directee, and the director in communion with one another as the directee grows in his or her relationship with God.

At other times, spiritual directors experience *desolation* or *resistance,* that is, a spontaneous *movement away from God* in that they feel dissonant with the directee's experience—emotionally distant, bored, frustrated, agitated, angry, anxious, or fearful, or they have little or no feeling at all. They might feel restless, become distracted, or have difficulty listening to and staying with the directee's experience. They may move away from a contemplative presence to a problem-solving, preaching, and advice-giving stance. They may feel unfocused or lost: how did we get here? where are we going? what am I doing? They may have lost sight of God's presence: where did you go, God? God is seemingly absent during the direction session. These countermovements can be very strong and obvious during a session or take place in a subtle way. Many times they occur without the directee's knowledge.

Countermovement occurs for a variety of reasons. First, the directee's resistance may be affecting the director. For example, after several months a directee still may not be taking the time to pray, causing the director to feel frustrated and annoyed. Second, the directee's growing intimacy with God may result in dissonant reactions within the director. For example, a directee may share with the director an image of being held by God; subsequently, the director spontaneously experiences an emotional distancing from both God and the directee. Third, an unresolved issue in the director may be touched. For instance, a directee who is confronting, through prayer, memories of emotional deprivation during childhood may remind the director of his or her own pain and darkness around a similar issue; therefore, the director struggles to stay connected interiorly with the directee's experience. Fourth, the director may experience a lack of freedom in a particular area of life, such as when the directee raises issues related to sexuality, and the director unconsciously withdraws because it produces discomfort. Finally, directors may experience a struggle in a particular direction relationship because of a relational dynamic such as countertransference. For example, a directee may remind the director of a significant person with whom the director is struggling, which interferes with the direction relationship and process.

Spiritual directors' interior movements form the primary foundation for developing a discerning heart. These movements, therefore, are the arena from which to explore the purposes, process, and skills of supervision.

Purposes of Supervision

The purposes of supervision are rooted in the spiritual director's experience of interior movements while in the process of directing. The overall goal of supervision is to help spiritual directors to grow in self-awareness and interior freedom in order to stay with directees' experiences and to be attentive to God during direction sessions. Specifically, this goal has three dimensions.

Exploring Interior Movements

Supervision strives to help spiritual directors to sift out their own interior movements that occur while they are directing. Thus they develop a keener sense of self-awareness.

Supervision helps spiritual directors to explore their own *dissonant experiences* of agitation, distraction, boredom, anxiety, fear, and anger (see the first case study in learning experience 6 in Part II). For example, a directee may feel God's intimate love while the director experiences agitation and envy. Or a directee may feel distant from God while the director becomes frustrated and impatient. Such dissonant interior reactions form the bulk of supervision.

Supervision also provides an arena for spiritual directors to notice and savor *consonant experiences* of joy, gratitude, peace, and love (see the second case study in learning experience 6 in Part II). For example, a directee may share a consoling experience of God while a director experiences a felt congruence with the directee by sharing feelings of peace, joy, and gratitude. This noticing and savoring experience during supervision helps directors to

- recognize, savor, and respond to their directees' experiences of God;

- develop an attitude of attentiveness to their own interior reactions to directees' experiences of God;

- create the inner space necessary for listening deeply to directees' experiences;

- assist directees to look closely at interior facts and share feelings with God;

- help directees linger with their experiences of God in life and prayer; and

- notice God's felt presence and/or lack of affective presence in the spiritual direction session itself.

Bringing Areas of Darkness into the Light

Supervision helps spiritual directors to bring into the light areas of resistance, affective attitudes, psychological and emotional blocks, areas of woundedness, and life struggles that prevent them from helping directees explore their life experience deeply or savor their experience of God fully. Through this uncovering of darkness and unfreedom, spiritual directors grow in deeper self-knowledge.

For example, a director can become restless as the directee shares the pain of a broken relationship because he or she also is coping with similar circumstances. Or a director may feel distant and bored when a directee describes intense pain regarding childhood abuse. Supervision can uncover the director's tendency to avoid dealing with one's own abuse issues as a child. Through supervision directors can explore vulnerable issues and hidden areas in order to

- grow more aware of the impact of unfree and resistant areas on themselves as persons and directors;

- release the binding and sometimes crippling power of these areas;

- bring these areas into conscious, affective relationship with God for their own personal and professional growth as spiritual directors;

- arrive at deeper and more nuanced self-understanding;

- recognize areas of weakness and strength in directing; and

- linger deeply with their directees' life and religious experience.

Growing in Interior Freedom
to Linger with Directees' Experiences

By exploring their interior movements and uncovering unresolved issues and unfree areas, spiritual directors create the inner space to be deeply present with directees. They grow in interior freedom. Their own inner space becomes uncluttered and spacious enough to be open and receptive to their directees. For instance, by discussing their frustration with their directees' resistance during supervision sessions, directors can grow more patient and accepting when their directees avoid God and prayer.

This growing inner freedom also enables directors to linger with their directees' experiences and stay with vulnerable issues. Directors can help their directees explore incidents of childhood abuse because, through supervision (and in other ways, too, such as counseling or Twelve-Step meetings), they can become more aware of their own family dysfunction. As beginning spiritual directors explore their hesitation or fear of helping their directees savor their experiences of God and uncover their desolations, they become freer to thoroughly explore their directees' experiences. This freedom helps spiritual directors to notice more keenly movements and counter-movements in their directees and to enjoy their directees' growing relationship with God.

Supervision, therefore, focuses primarily on the interior movements of spiritual directors that are stirred and the areas of unfreedom that emerge during direction sessions in order to help them grow in greater self-awareness and freedom. As this happens, they are better able to stay with their directees' experiences.

Supervision sometimes addresses the experience of directees in order to help directors understand their own reactions more clearly and attain a greater clarity about interior movements in directees. Still, the primary focus remains the inner experience of spiritual directors.

The Supervisor's Stance

Supervisors are *companions* for spiritual directors, accompanying them on their journey toward interior awareness and personal freedom. They are *codiscerners* with spiritual directors as they grow in their ability to sift through their own interior movements that occur during direction experiences and as they develop a discerning heart. Further, supervisors are also a *contemplative presence,* inviting directors to look at how God is present during direction sessions, to savor God's affective presence, and to explore God's seeming absence. They are *reverent evokers* who assist spiritual directors in discovering their own inner truth, both the darkness and the light. They also act as a *resting place* for spiritual directors in times of discouragement, a supportive presence as they work through areas of weakness and feelings of inadequacy. Finally, they are *skilled helpers* who facilitate spiritual directors in their ability to listen more fully, savor more deeply, and embrace more completely their directees' life and God experiences.

Clarifying the Meaning of Supervision

The term *supervision* can evoke certain images in people. In the workplace supervision often involves teaching people how to perform certain tasks or telling employees what to do and how to do it. Supervisors are perceived as overseers whose main function is to assure that a job is done properly and efficiently. In the helping professions, such as counseling or social work, people may think of supervision as consulting about a certain situation: the focus is on a particular case, not the helping person's experience of the case. In its purest sense, however, supervision focuses primarily on the helping person's inner experience and responses.

Clarifying what supervision of spiritual directors is *not* can facilitate a more precise understanding of what it is. Supervision of spiritual directors is not one of guiding the tasks of spiritual direction, although the spiritual director will be learning direction skills through the supervision process. Supervision is not primarily overseeing the work of the spiritual director, although the supervisor must have a good sense of the quality of spiritual direction being done. Supervision is not consulting about the directee's situation, although occasionally a director will need to consult with an experienced director or supervisor to discuss how to handle certain situations, such as depression in a directee or how to work with someone who has been sexually abused. Supervision is not a teaching experience in the sense that the supervisor instructs a person how to handle certain situations or explains how to stay with a directee's experience. However, "teachable moments" can occur during the flow of supervision. Supervision is not therapy, although personal issues will be explored and much healing and new insights into oneself will emerge through the process of staying focused on the director's experience.

To reiterate, supervision is the processing of the inner experiences of spiritual directors that are evoked during direction sessions in order to help them grow in awareness of their reactions and responses, to allow them to respond in a God-centered and interiorly free manner, and to maintain a contemplative focus. Other tasks and benefits may occur through supervision, such as guiding, consulting, teaching, and personal healing; however, these are secondary tasks and occur only after the primary purpose is served.

Conclusion

The experience of supervision is both a gift and a challenge for spiritual directors. It is a gift in that it enables directors to be attentive to God's presence during direction sessions, in touch with the variety and richness of interior movements in themselves and their directees, and aware of areas within that prevent them from staying with their directees' experiences. Supervison is a challenge in that it requires a precise understanding of its purposes, a constant prayerful attitude on the part of the director and the supervisor, a clear focus on the director's experience and the experience of God, a deep honesty about one's strengths and weaknesses, and a willingness to explore one's vulnerable issues and areas of unfreedom. As both a gift and a challenge supervision is an essential process in order for individuals to develop as discerning, free, and caring spiritual directors.

Questions for Reflection and Discussion

For Supervisors

1. Of the assumptions in spiritual direction and supervision that apply, which are most striking to you? Would you add any assumptions?

2. The three overall purposes of supervision are (1) exploring interior movements of spiritual directors; (2) bringing their areas of darkness into the light; and (3) encouraging directors' growth in interior freedom in order to linger with directees' experiences. How do these purposes relate to your idea and experience of offering supervision? Give examples.

3. Describe your awareness of God during supervision sessions. Do you see supervision as an encounter with a

trinitarian God—that is, as a threefold experience of communion of you, the director, and God?

4. Describe your presence during supervision. Are you a companion? a codiscerner? a reverent evoker? a contemplative presence? a resting place? a skilled helper? a teacher? Which of these stances apply in your approach to supervision? Which do you need to develop?

5. What are your notions and images of supervision? How have they influenced your approach to the supervision of spiritual directors?

For Spiritual Directors

1. Which of the purposes of spiritual direction speak most to your experience of offering direction?

2. How do contemplative and discernment skills apply in your ministry of spiritual direction? Give examples.

3. How aware are you of your own interior movements while directing? What has helped you to become more aware?

4. What insights have you gained about yourself, your directees, and God through your experience of interior movements during direction sessions?

5. How does your experience of being supervised help you to explore your interior movements, bring hidden areas into the open, and grow in interior freedom? Give examples of each.

6. What are your supervisor's usual stances in supervision? What do you find helpful and/or unhelpful about each of these stances?

7. Do you and your supervisor(s) share a common understanding about supervising spiritual directors? Have you

clarified your understanding with one another at the beginning of a given supervision commitment? What could happen (or has happened) if you do not have a common perspective on the focus and purposes of supervision?

A Contemplative Moment

Enter into your interior space. Notice the darkness, the blocks, the brokenness. Ask God to hold these dark realities and help you to hold them with reverence and care. Feel God's tender touch and reverent embrace transform your blocks and brokenness. Let the living waters of God's love wash over them.

Notice, too, the growing freedom in your interior space—not a freedom that dismisses brokenness but a freedom that embraces your broken places and transforms you into a wounded healer.

Thank God for the darkness and the light, the woundedness and wholeness, that reside within you. Thank God for embracing and dwelling in both.

See your interior space being transformed into a warm home and a safe resting place for others.

Prayer for Inner Freedom

God of life-giving freedom, thank you for the privilege of being with people in such a vulnerable way as they share their brokenness as well as their giftedness, their darkness as well as their light.

I ask for the grace of awareness of my own brokenness and darkness. Give me a willing and courageous spirit to delve deeply into my own vulnerability, so that I can be freely with others in their woundedness.

Help me to see my areas of darkness so that these can come out into the light, to explore my brokenness so that it can bask in your healing touch, to become aware of my resistances so that they can be freed by your loving Spirit.

Create an open space within me so that I can receive others' brokenness and vulnerability with tenderness and love.

Help me to be a resting place where others can bring their struggles as well as their joys.

Let me find a home in you so others can find a home in me.

Thank you, God, for the inner freedom growing within me that allows others to encounter your loving presence.

2

Direction Experiences to Bring to Supervision: The Content of Supervision

The experience of supervision can be compared to the story of Jesus with the woman at the well (Jn 4:4–30). Just as Jesus and the woman peered into the well of her life experience and her heart, so, too, the supervisor, Jesus, and the spiritual director look into the well of the director's interior space while directing. Having a contemplative presence, they look with reverence and care. They draw out the living waters of spiritual direction encounters. They sift out and embrace the director's inner realities that are revealed through contemplative gazing and reverent unfolding.

Chapter 2 addresses two questions: What types of experiences and situations do spiritual directors bring to supervision? How do spiritual directors know which ones to bring to a given session? The experiences will be discussed in relation to five areas: (1) the experience of interior movements; (2) the director's personal issues that are stirred during direction sessions; (3) moral, theological, spiritual, and cultural differences; (4) the development of a contemplative attitude and approach; and (5) the relationship between the director and directee. These areas are also outlined in learning experience 3.

Although these five areas will be examined separately, they can be experienced simultaneously. For instance, as directors explore their struggles to stay with directees' experiences of God in a contemplative way, they may discover that a personal, vulnerable issue prevents them from doing so. Therefore the starting point of the supervision session can begin with the development of a contemplative attitude; however, a significant part of the session could be devoted to an issue of vulnerability and how it affects the director's ability to be contemplative.

The Experience of Interior Movements

As explained in chapter 1, spiritual directors experience a variety of interior movements while they companion others. Interior movements form the foundation of spiritual direction, that is, all of a director's experiences are in some way grounded in the experience of God and the resulting affective reactions. The rhythm of movement and countermovement in a direction session can involve any of the following dynamics:

Directee	Director
Movement	Movement
Movement	Countermovement
Countermovement	Movement
Countermovement	Countermovement

During supervision sessions spiritual directors may need to process direction experiences that reflect any of these four dynamics.

Movement Evokes Movement

The first dynamic of movement evoking movement occurs when the directee's consoling experience of God and interior movements of joy, peace, or love stirs a consoling movement in the director. During these often deep and sacred moments the director experiences communion with God and the directee. They feel a sensation of being on "holy ground." Both the directee and director are savoring consolation. It is important for a director to bring such an experience to supervision for several reasons:

- The director wants help in staying with the directee's experience of God and assistance in being contemplative so that the directee can unfold the richness of the experience.

- The director wants to savor God's affective presence in a session in order to be able to notice and savor God's presence in future sessions.

- The director wants assistance improving contemplative skills, that is, the ability to help a directee linger longer with a particular experience of God.

Movement Evokes Countermovement

The second dynamic of movement evoking countermovement occurs when the directee's consoling experience of God precipitates resistance in the director, such as when a directee shares an intimate experience of God and the director becomes emotionally distant, or when a directee shares an overwhelming experience of God's love and the director feels envy and resentment.

Directors process these countermovements in order to notice and explore underlying issues so that their countermovements do not interfere with the savoring of the directee's experiences of God.

Countermovement Evokes Movement

The third dynamic of countermovement evoking movement takes place when a directee's countermovement leads to a consoling experience in the director; that is, when the directee experiences resistance in prayer, the director experiences consolation and remains affectively connected with God. The directee may lose sight of God, both in prayer and in life, but the director stays in tune with God during the direction session. For example, a directee is avoiding God in prayer because of a painful loss, and the director is patient and accepting of the directee's resistance. The director brings this situation to supervision to learn how to cope better with the directee's ongoing resistance.

Another example can occur when the directee experiences moderate depression and spiritual desolation over a period of time and the director consistently prays not only for the directee but also for him- or herself. Through avid prayer the director is able to maintain a close connection with God. The director may bring this to supervision to deepen the sense of God as a companion, to savor God's strength in order to continue helping the directee in a caring manner, and to gain insight into working with a directee suffering from depression and spiritual desolation.

Countermovement Evokes Countermovement

The fourth dynamic of countermovement evoking countermovement occurs when the directee's resistance precipitates desolate feelings in the director, such as when the directee does not pray and the director becomes frustrated. The director wants to process these feelings of frustration in order to work with the directee's resistance in a reverent and contemplative way. Other times the directee may avoid deep feelings, and the director becomes bored, struggling to stay in the moment with the directee. Through supervision the director can learn to be fully present with the directee and discover how to move the directee toward a deeper experience.

In sum, supervision assists spiritual directors to be *aware of* and, eventually, *understand* the rhythm of their interior movements in a given direction session. Recognizing their own interior reactions while directing allows them to be less self-absorbed and be more attentive to others and to God. The more self-aware and less self-absorbed they are, the more other-absorbed they become—absorbed, that is, in their directees' experiences and in God's presence. Thus, spiritual directors' inner awareness allows them to stay connected with directees' experiences of God and discern how to help them savor, explore, and discover their experiences.

The Spiritual Director's Personal Issues

Another set of experiences that spiritual directors bring to supervision are those in which a personal unresolved issue or unhealed area emerges during a direction session. The director may have a strong affective reaction to something the directee shares, or avoids an issue that the directee needs to discuss. The director then realizes an area of unfreedom within oneself is being touched upon. This dynamic can be experienced in two ways.

Areas of Unfreedom, Vulnerability, and/or Brokenness

At times a directee's behavior affects an area of unfreedom, vulnerability, and brokenness or touches on the shadow side of the director. Consider the following examples:

- The directee is in intense pain; the director has a tendency to want to rescue the directee from suffering and recognizes that this tendency could occur in similar situations.

- The directee expresses anger at God and other people; the director has a tendency to smooth things over and minimize the intensity of the directee's anger.

- The directee talks incessantly, which threatens the director's self-worth and makes the director feel unimportant.

- The directee, though prayerful and in touch with God, does not pray daily at a regular time, which affects the director's perfectionism and need for order.

Spiritual directors need to address these situations to process their vulnerable issues and to see how these issues affect their work with a directee. Further, by doing so, they will gain more insight and freedom, which will enable them to be more fully present in all direction situations.

Mirroring Dynamic ("Parallel Process")

A mirroring dynamic takes place when a director is undergoing or struggling with a similar situation or issue as the directee, and the director notices strong inner reactions or a tendency to move away from the directee's sharing. That is, the director's life or inner experience is being "mirrored" by the directee's exterior and interior struggles. In counseling circles this dynamic is referred to as *parallel process*. Some examples of this mirroring dynamic follow.

- A directee is coping with the loss of a very close friend, which elicits feelings of loss in the director regarding a similar situation.

- A directee struggles with a codependent tendency to be a people-pleaser and obtain peace at any cost; the director also experiences this struggle and thus tends to avoid the issue altogether.

- A directee is struggling with intimacy issues, which evokes fearful feelings in the director, who also has trouble being intimate and vulnerable with God and others.

- A directee is trying to control a compulsive tendency to overeat, which triggers similar feelings in the director and the director's unresolved addiction to food.

Do supervision sessions take on the nature of counseling sessions when the director's own personal issues are explored? Although supervision can be therapeutic and liberating and can help heal directors' unresolved issues, it does not qualify as counseling because directors only process the personal issues that affect the direction process. If directors do not process these issues through supervision or in other productive ways, then such issues can circumvent the direction process altogether and prevent the director from thoroughly exploring significant issues of the directee. Directors need to bring to supervision the real matter of their inner beings because it is these matters that influence the depth and quality of their direction sessions.

Moral, Theological, Spiritual, and Cultural Differences

Another set of experiences that spiritual directors bring to supervision relate to differences in morality, theology, spirituality, and culture. That is, the discrepancy between a director's moral, spiritual, or theological perspective on an issue or cultural background may be quite considerable and can create turmoil in the director. The following examples illustrate how significant differences between director and directee affect the spiritual director.

Discrepancy in Moral Beliefs

At times directees may be dealing with a personal issue that has significant moral overtones. Their beliefs and potential behavior can precipitate a disturbance within their directors. Some examples include the following:

- A directee, a married Episcopalian priest, is having an affair with a married woman in his parish. He rationalizes his actions during spiritual direction, which causes an inner conflict in the director, who believes the priest's behavior is morally wrong and abusive toward the woman.

- A directee, who is a member of a denomination that accepts a woman's right to choose to have an abortion, becomes pregnant. The directee and her husband have marital difficulties, and she herself has some serious health problems. In spiritual direction she considers the possibility of having an abortion. The director, who believes abortion is immoral and experiences deep anguish, needs to decide whether to continue seeing this woman for direction.

Differences in Theology and Spirituality

At times directors' and directees' theological beliefs and approaches to spirituality are so diverse that the spiritual direction relationship is significantly affected. Therefore, directors need to process these differences to see how they affect the spiritual direction experience. Consider the following examples:

- A directee's experience of God is primarily a feminine one in which God is both mother and female friend. This experience precipitates feelings of irritation and insecurity in the director, who accepts God only from a masculine perspective.

- The directee, a permanent deacon in the Roman Catholic Church, is very traditional and disapproves of women becoming involved in liturgies. The director, who strongly favors equality of women in all arenas of life, experiences deep distress and anger toward the deacon.

- A directee's approach to God is strongly charismatic, which makes the director, who had a difficult experience with a group of charismatics, uncomfortable.

- A directee, deeply rooted in the Carmelite tradition, is accustomed to praying without images. On the other hand, the director's approach to spirituality is mostly grounded in the Ignatian tradition of imaged experiences of God. Thus the director feels insecure and inadequate.

Cultural Differences

Cultural differences between directors and directees are often related to ethnic backgrounds, work experiences, and living situations.

- A director offers spiritual direction to people who have come from an oppressive Central American country. The director experiences strong repulsive and fearful feelings regarding the violent circumstances from which they escaped and needs to process these feelings.

- A director, deeply committed to working with the poor, struggles with a directee who is very wealthy and has little social awareness.

- A directee is deeply committed to working with prisoners. The director begins to notice subtle feelings of prejudice and anger toward the criminals, which interferes with the ability to be fully present during the direction session.

As directors process their feelings regarding their directees' different moral, theological, spiritual, or cultural backgrounds, they gain deeper insight into their own beliefs and grow in the freedom to help their directees process their experiences. On the other hand, they may realize that the differences are so great that they cannot direct such individuals. Whatever the outcome, they often feel freer and more confident to make choices for the well-being of the directee.

A Contemplative Attitude and Approach

Spiritual directors also bring to supervision experiences and issues directly related to the process of spiritual direction, such as the struggle to develop a contemplative approach, weaknesses and feelings of inadequacy as a spiritual director, and significant breakthroughs in learning the spiritual direction process. The following are key situations and examples of each.

Developing a Contemplative Attitude

The director may become aware that God's presence is not felt nor being attended to adequately during direction sessions. The directee's relationship with God has become secondary to discussion of other aspects of one's life. Thus the sessions resemble counseling sessions too closely, focusing only on the directee's life experience and struggles. This loss of focus can manifest itself in various ways:

- A director talks too much and works too hard with a directee.

- A director falls into problem-solving or advice-giving approaches.

- A director becomes bored and frustrated with the sessions

because he or she becomes entangled in the same struggle as the directee, such as a difficult marriage relationship.

Directors bring these situations to supervision in order to process their feelings, to gain more insight into a specific dynamic, to become freer from certain dynamics, and to discover ways to bring the focus back to the directee's growth in relationship with God.

Shortcomings or Vulnerable Areas as a Spiritual Director and Feelings of Inadequacy

As spiritual directors begin their journey as a companion to others, they may experience strong feelings of inadequacy. They may also discover shortcomings that affect the quality of spiritual direction. Some examples follow.

- A director finds it difficult to listen from the heart, approaching spiritual direction too much from an intellectual perspective. Therefore the director misses important interior movements in the directee.

- A director struggles with being in touch with one's feelings and therefore finds it difficult to help others explore their feelings.

- A beginning director feels inadequate while savoring directees' experiences of God and exploring their countermovements. The director brings these feelings to supervision in order to gain inner freedom and a sense of confidence in staying with people's experiences.

- A directee, a young woman, shares her story of being sexually abused. The director feels uncomfortable and inadequate dealing with this issue. The director discusses the direction experience in supervision in order to explore what lies beneath these uncomfortable feelings and to discover ways of handling the area of sexual abuse.

Through supervision, directors process vulnerable areas and inadequate feelings to gain insight, grow in freedom to stay with directees' experiences, and improve the overall quality of their ministry of companioning others.

Significant Breakthroughs

After a great deal of work spiritual directors may come to understand a certain spiritual direction dynamic or experience a significant breakthrough in a difficult area. During supervision they may wish to explore a new insight or celebrate a long-awaited discovery.

- A spiritual director understands experientially what it means to be a companion, not a problem solver.

- After months of slipping into a teaching role in direction sessions, a director feels what it is like to be truly evocative, that is, helping a directee savor an experience of God rather than giving instructions on how to pray.

- A director who has had a heady approach to spiritual direction concretely experiences the benefits of helping a directee focus on affective experiences of God rather than on beliefs about God.

- A director, uncertain about following the call to be a spiritual director, experiences strong confirmation during a session.

Exploring, savoring, and celebrating these new insights can help directors deepen the new understandings and discover ways to put breakthroughs into concrete practice.

The Relationship between Director and Directee

As in any significant relationship, relational dynamics occur between the director and directee. These dynamics may include feeling connected or unconnected with each other, admiring some traits but disliking other traits about each other, and projecting onto each other. When director and directee experience any relational dynamic that interferes with the direction encounter and the contemplative focus, they need to bring the dynamics of the relationship to supervision. Below are three key relational issues that may arise during sessions.

A Significant Struggle in the Director-Directee Relationship

As the direction relationship deepens, strong feelings—either negative or positive—may develop in the director, directee, or both parties:

- A directee begins to fall in love with the director, or vice versa.

- One feels strong sexual feelings for the other, or they both feel a growing sexual attraction toward each other.

- Both the director and directee notice that a friendship is forming between them. They need to make a decision as to how they want to continue their relationship—either as a direction relationship or as a friendship.

- A director feels controlled or dominated by a directee.

- A director feels intense anger because of a directee's manipulative and passive/aggressive ways.

Intense and conflicting feelings must be processed during supervision to dissipate their power and to explore their root cause, to maintain the sacredness of the direction process, and to decide what actions need to be taken to honor faithfully the director-directee relationship and the direction covenant.

Issues of Transference and Countertransference

Directees may experience *transference;* directors *countertransference,* which means that one or the other projects feelings or attitudes from a past relationship (usually a parental relationship) onto the other. Although this dynamic often happens unconsciously, the person may become aware of it through reflection. Some instances of countertransference are the following:

- A director becomes fearful of the directee, who resembles the director's father and who reminds the director of the difficulty within the parent-child relationship.

- A directee resembles the director's mother. The director's mother relationship is a close one. Thus the director struggles with strong feelings of enmeshment, even losing a sense of objectivity during the direction sessions.

- A director feels strong feelings of anger toward a directee, even though the directee is a very pleasant person. The director knows the anger is caused by an internal struggle, not by the directee's behavior.

Examples of transference:

- For no apparent reason a directee becomes fearful of a director, accusing the director of being pushy. The director needs to process confused or hurt feelings that may emerge and determine the best approach to take.

- A directee, a young woman, begins to call and visit the director's office and buys the director gifts. The director, an older woman, suspects that the directee sees her as the mother she never had. The director needs to process her uncomfortable feelings and gain a sense of direction about what to do about the directee's behavior.

- A directee accuses the director of having certain attitudes and behaviors that the director knows are not true, provoking much anxiety within the director.

Processing transference and countertransference experiences during supervision sessions enables directors to gain deeper insight into themselves and past relationships. It also helps to keep the direction relationship "clean"—that is, free from any bias—and it seeks to regain a contemplative focus and discern what steps to take in certain situations.

A Painful Termination of a Direction Relationship

At times a painful termination to a direction relationship results, either by the director, the directee, or both persons. Supervision can help the director to (1) explore issues and reasons for the termination as well as understand one's feelings; (2) examine how the termination occurred, that is, whether it was done in an adequate and thorough manner; and (3) gain insight into how to handle future terminations, whether painful or not.

Deciding Which Situation to Bring to a Supervision Session

To help the supervision process in an ongoing way, spiritual directors can use several practices to facilitate their awareness of their own interior space while directing. One practice is prayerful, sensitive, and consistent self-reflection—that is, the process of self-supervision. Second, pray before, during, and after direction sessions for the gift of a discerning heart in order to be sensitive and open to the spirits—one's own spirit, the directee's spirit, and God's Spirit. Third, be aware of and continuously work through personal issues, struggles, and resistances and seek counseling when "stuck" in an unresolved issue. Fourth, be attentive to one's own interior movements through spiritual direction. Engaging in these four practices regularly will also help directors decide which of their experiences to bring to supervision.

How exactly does a spiritual director decide which situation to bring to a supervision session? This dilemma can be explored through the heart and mind of a particular spiritual director. Sharon, in the second year of a training program for spiritual directors, attends a two-hour individual supervision session every other week. During a two-week period she has had ten direction sessions. Now she sits down to ponder: What session would be most helpful to process in supervision? What session would offer the likelihood of a good *verbatim*— that is, a word-for-word account of the director-directee conversation? She prayerfully browses through her spiritual direction log (see learning experience 1), which contains the

ten sessions and attempts to acknowledge certain feelings—
her strongest interior movement, for example, a struggle she
has experienced with a directee regarding the direction relationship, or any unfree area within herself that was being
stirred. With Jesus, she contemplatively looks into the well of
her ten direction experiences, trying to discern which one to
explore at length through supervision.

Sharon is aware of experiences that have been processed
in other sessions and tries not to continuously bring the same-
type situation or the same directee into the process unless it is
a particularly challenging situation that needs a great deal of
attention. She has already prayed with each of these ten sessions, leaving a half hour after each session to write in her log
and to pray. As she looks into the well of these ten sessions
she asks herself a series of questions:

- During which session did I experience the strongest interior movements? What were they? Were they consoling or
  desolating movements? Do I know fully what lay beneath
  a desolating movement, or would it be helpful to explore
  this during supervision?

- During any session were any of my unfree areas or vulnerable issues precipitated? What was that area or issue?
  What were some of the feelings stirred? Did this experience interfere with my staying with the directee? Do I
  need to explore this area in supervision to gain more
  insight and freedom around it so it does not interfere
  with my ability to be a spiritual companion to this
  directee as well as others?

- Were there any sessions in which I experienced inner
  conflict over moral or theological beliefs? struggled with
  someone's approach to spirituality? felt out of touch with
  someone's cultural experience?

- Did any of my weaknesses as a spiritual director manifest
  themselves in any of these sessions? any session where I
  was struggling to stay with a directee's life or religious
  experience? any session in which I was struggling to

keep a contemplative atmosphere and focus? Are sessions too much resembling counseling situations? Have we turned to problem solving, for example?

Sharon continues to ask these questions during her prayerful reflection until she sifts out the most important direction experience to bring to her next supervision session. This experience will help her deepen self-awareness and allow her to continue to refine her development as a spiritual director.

Conclusion

One of the gifts of supervision is to be able to spend time delving deeply into a direction experience to discover what motivates the spiritual director's various affective reactions. During a supervision session—as the director, supervisor, and God look contemplatively into the director's well of direction experiences—they lower the bucket into the well and draw out a direction experience. In a reverent way they process a situation, thoroughly knowing that this experience has ramifications for one's total development as a spiritual director. They savor the living waters of God's presence. Thus supervision offers the sacred opportunity for the spiritual director to drink of God's love, experiencing Jesus' promise: "The water I give shall become a fountain within you, leaping up to provide God's life" (Jn 4:14).

Questions for Reflection and Discussion

For Supervisors

1. Reflect on the situations/experiences that spiritual directors have brought to you during supervision. What kinds of dynamics and experiences are involved? Do they tend to bring the same situations time after time? If so, what can you do about this?

2. What are some of the values of bringing a variety of direction situations to supervision? How can you help those you supervise to see these values?

3. Reflect on the ways that you help spiritual directors delve into the various dynamics mentioned in this chapter. What are some concrete ways that you have helped them in their exploration? Can you think of sessions when you were particularly helpful?

4. Reflect on a time when a spiritual director brought a situation in which two or more of the dynamics described in this chapter applied, such as when a mirroring dynamic occurred, an area of vulnerability took place in the director, or an area of strong resistance emerged. How did you handle this supervision session? Where did you begin? Did you deal with all the areas, or just focus on one?

For Spiritual Directors

1. What types of situations/experiences do you bring to supervision? Do you tend to bring the same type of situation, or do you bring a variety of experiences?

2. What advantages do you see in bringing different direction situations to supervision? What can you do to help yourself become more aware of introducing variety to the sessions?

3. Remember a supervision session in which you brought a particularly difficult situation to supervision. Which

situations or dynamics occurred? What happened during and as a result of supervision?

4. Do you take the time to pray over your direction sessions? What has happened as a result of your prayerful attitude? What has happened because of a lack of it?

5. Do you take the time to prayerfully reflect on which direction session to bring to supervision? What are the advantages of doing this? What could happen, or has happened, when you do not take the time to consider which direction session to process during supervision?

6. Do you keep a spiritual direction log? If so, how have you found this helpful? If not, what tool do you use to keep track of your directees' experiences and pray with them?

A Contemplative Moment

As you sit in God's loving presence, let the waters of God's love surround you, wash over you, and embrace you.

Ask God to wash away the blindness of your eyes, your heart, and your mind so that you can see yourself and others as God sees you and others, especially during the sacred encounters of spiritual direction and supervision.

Ask God to reveal and transform any blind spots that prevent you from facing the truth in yourself, or that prevent you from helping others to face their inner truth. If a particular blind spot comes to mind, invite God to wash away the darkness and reveal the light of truth.

Prayer for Truth and Enlightenment

God of truth, enlighten my mind and heart to see your truth and my truth. Help me to see that your primary truth is that of overflowing love—that your abundant love embraces both darkness and light, pain and joy, fear and courage, weakness and strength, life and death.

I ask for the grace to see my truth in you—to see my darkness and my light, my fears and my courage, my pain and my joy, my self-hatred and my self-acceptance through your loving gaze. For in seeing myself as you see me, I will be given the light to see others through your eyes.

Give me an embracing heart like yours—a heart that embraces my sinfulness, my brokenness, and my vulnerability as you embrace them. For in embracing myself as you embrace me, I will be able to embrace others in the totality of their truth.

Thank you, God of light, for enlightening my mind to see divine truth and human realness.

Thank you, God of life, for encouraging me to embrace all aspects of life in myself, in others, and in you.

A Contemplative Presence and an Evocative Approach: The Process of Supervision

The supervision process for spiritual directors parallels the spiritual direction process in many ways. Since God's presence is vital for both supervision and spiritual direction, the approach and process of supervision is contemplative and evocative. Taking a contemplative and evocative approach enables spiritual directors to develop a discerning heart: to be attentive to and sift out their interior movements so that they can enter into their directees' experiences. This chapter describes a contemplative and evocative supervision process and provides examples.

Looking into the Well

Imagine a supervisor and a spiritual director are with Jesus at the well. All three gaze into the well of the director's interior life. They look into the director's interior direction space on a regular basis, possibly once a week during the period of a year. Lowering the bucket into his or her interior space and taking hold of a direction experience, they process the experience during a supervision session, contemplating it both in itself and in relation to the director's other direction experiences, personal struggles, and life circumstances. For instance, as a supervisor and director explore a direction session in which a directee is praying over the loss of a special friend, they may discover unresolved aspects of the director's grief.

What do the spiritual director, supervisor, and God notice as they explore a particular direction experience? At first they see only surface ripples (initial reactions); then they witness pure and polluted realities (deep harmonizing feelings and strong dissonant attitudes). As they stay with these contrasting feelings, they see the bottom of the well—that is, unresolved issues and areas of unfreedom. They explore these issues and areas, drawing them out reverently and caringly, striving to gain more insight. Finally, they enjoy the touch of the water. They savor the growing self-knowledge and freedom that results from gazing into the well and embracing the realities within. From this experience they realize that the water in the well is the living water of God's presence.

Thus, the rhythm of supervision enables pure areas of light and polluted areas of darkness to emerge into the director's awareness. This process in turn facilitates the discernment of interior movements and growth in inner freedom. The process is both contemplative and evocative.

A *contemplative presence* refers to a reverent attentiveness to the spiritual director's experiences and God's presence. An atmosphere is created in which such attentiveness can take place. An *evocative approach* means that supervisors can help reveal directors' interior experiences in a free-flowing and open-ended way. Supervisors assist them in discovering their interior realities through an exploratory, revelatory approach. The basic principle at work here is that feelings have greater power and insights deeper impact when a director discovers something for him- or herself—albeit with the help of a supervisor—rather than the supervisor pointing the way. By exploring spiritual directors' inner experience in an evocative way, supervisors can help them become aware of their blind spots.

Supervision must be primarily contemplative and evocative in order for spiritual directors to develop a discerning heart. Therefore they can more readily identify their areas of strength and growth, discover their areas of resistance and struggle, explore and embrace vulnerable issues and unresolved conflicts, and integrate new insights into other direction situations. Supervisors can then provide feedback and underscore significant insights at the end of the supervision session.

In sum, by a contemplative presence and an evocative approach, supervision strives to assist the spiritual director to

- *notice initial reactions* at a given moment in the direction session (for example, "I feel anxious.");

- *explore deeper feelings and attitudes* that lie beneath a reaction ("I feel overwhelmed . . . helpless . . . out of control . . . ");

- *uncover and embrace experiential reasons* underneath the feelings—areas of brokenness, unfreedom, unresolved conflicts ("I feel overwhelmed when Sarah is processing her midlife crisis because I am also in the midst of a painful one");

- *grow in self-awareness and freedom* ("I feel freer and more alive now having become aware of my helplessness and feelings of inadequacy and the reasons for these intense feelings");

- *recognize differences* in oneself that result from sharing difficult emotions ("I feel different now about Sarah's midlife experience. Having seen what was underneath my overwhelmed and helpless feelings, I feel freer and more able to help Sarah, and others, explore their midlife losses and other painful struggles");

- *be attentive to God's felt presence or absence* during a direction session ("God's presence was so alive and vibrant as I helped Sarah savor her experience of God as she works through her midlife struggle. . . . When I got stuck in my helpless feelings I lost sight of God's presence. I became paralyzed, and God got pushed to the background"); and

- *apply insights and learnings* gained from supervision to specific direction sessions ("Having talked out your fears and feelings of helplessness and inadequacy here, how might you respond now to Sarah when she talks about a particular midlife pain? Let's role-play how the conversation might unfold").

Reactions, Reasons, and Results

The unfolding process of supervision focuses on three R's: reactions, reasons, and results.

Reactions

During spiritual direction sessions, directors experience various reactions. Sometimes they will connect with their directees' experiences; they may feel peace, joy, life, compassion, empathy, or unity with God, for example. At other times, however, they will feel out of touch with directees—distant, bored, frustrated, agitated, anxious, angry, or fearful of their experiences. During supervision they can become aware of deeper feelings, attitudes, and beliefs. For instance, a director's initial reaction may be frustration, and by staying with this frustration, he or she may notice feelings of inadequacy or the development of a perfectionistic attitude.

Reasons

By noticing various reactions and staying with deeper feelings, underlying reasons for these reactions can surface. They are not reasons of analysis but rather *reasons of experience* and are revealed through feelings, reactions, and attitudes. They represent past and present experiences that can prevent a director from connecting with a directee because of unresolved conflicts or areas of brokenness and unfreedom. These areas apply usually because of the director's particular experiences in life. For example, a directee may pray to come to terms with an experience of emotional abandonment by a workaholic father. Meanwhile, the director's strong feelings emerge based on a similar experience.

Results

By noticing various reactions and recognizing underlying reasons, spiritual directors can experience powerful results. They gain a more nuanced self-knowledge as persons and as directors. In essence they become interiorly free. Unfelt and repressed feelings are experienced, and hidden issues are brought out into the open and embraced in a caring way. They often feel different at the end of a supervision session: more aware, free, confident, and open. This growing freedom and confidence overflows into future direction sessions in specific ways: directors' inner space is more receptive to their directee's experiences. Further their verbal responses become more appropriate.

Examples of the Supervision Process

Example 1: Underlying Feelings of Inadequacy

Directee's sharing: "Not much happened in prayer these past few weeks. Actually, I didn't pray much at all. I couldn't get myself down to it."

Director's initial reaction (unspoken): frustration (countermovement evokes countermovement)

Discovered through supervision:
    Through an evocative approach the supervisor helps the director to uncover the following feelings:

Director's reactions	Reasons
Frustration	Directee isn't praying.
Anger	The directee has been in resistance for several months.
Helplessness	I'm not sure what to do. I feel out of control.
Inadequacy	Probably another director could do a better job.

Results

The director grows more aware of feelings and inner reasons that can "hook" him or her. This awareness prevents similar situations from occurring in subsequent sessions and allows greater patience to address the directee's resistance.

Example 2: Fear of Intimacy

Directee's sharing: "I felt God holding me."

Director's initial reaction: anxiety (movement evokes counter-movement)

Discovered through supervision:

Director's reactions	Reasons
Anxiety	It feels too intimate to me.
Fear	I'm afraid of being held sometimes.
Fear	I'm uncomfortable with my own sexual feelings.
Anger	The nuns in school taught us such distorted things about sex that made us fearful.
Joy	I'm glad to be aware of this.

Results

By recognizing the feelings and reasons that evoke anxiety, the director attempts to take concrete action in order to feel more comfortable with intimate experiences of God—that is, understand the beauty and goodness of sexuality. The director is able to gain the inner freedom to stay in tune emotionally and verbally with the directee's intimate experience of God.

Example 3: Uncompleted Grieving (Mirroring Dynamic and Vulnerable Area)

Directee's sharing: "My father is getting closer and closer to death" (cries).

Director's initial reaction: Agitation

Discovered through supervision:

Director's reactions	Reasons
Agitation and restlessness	Too intense when she cries.
Anger	I'm angry because her father's been sick for so long. Why doesn't God take him?
Sadness	"Jane" has been through so much.
Pain (cries)	I went through something similar with my mother, but I thought I had worked through this.
Anger	I'm still angry at God about it.
Surprise and gratefulness	I didn't realize I was still so angry at God about my mother's illness. I need to deal with this some more in prayer.

Results

The director is able to be more fully present with the directee next time she shares painful memories about her father. She does not move her directee away from her pain, which is what she initially was doing because of her own unresolved anger with God. She now realizes the need for more personal prayer.

Example 4: Changing Self-Identity (Mirroring Dynamic)

Directee's sharing: "Now I can see that I'm being called to get in touch with who I am and who the Lord is in my life. All my life I've been doing for others and I don't regret that, but I don't know who I really am."

Director's initial reaction: Sadness

Discovered through supervision:

Director's reactions	Reasons
Sadness	I'm going through the same thing.
Compassion	I know how hard it is.
Anger	Why has it taken me so long to face my parents' alcoholism? I'm forty-eight years old!
Overwhelmed	It's so painful letting my controlling self die and my vulnerable self come alive.
Empathy	I feel such a oneness with "Tom."

Results

The director experiences deep compassion for the directee, who is undergoing a painful experience. This enables the director to linger more fully with him. The director realizes how much more work needs to be done and recognizes, too, the necessity for a greater awareness of God.

Conclusion

As the supervisor, spiritual director, and Jesus look into the well, the richness and depth, the struggle and freedom of the spiritual director's interior life unfolds. This gazing is done in God's presence, which allows inner truths to reveal themselves in a caring and contemplative atmosphere. It is God who guides the revelation of unfree areas. It is God who brings darkness into the light and purifies the polluted waters. This self-revelation enables the waters of the spiritual director's inner space to become clear, sparkling, and receptive to the living water of God's presence in direction sessions.

Questions for Reflection and Discussion

For Supervisors

1. How does the looking into the well analogy of the director's interior space resonate with your idea and experience of supervision?

2. How is your approach to supervision contemplative? Describe a few contemplative moments in supervision. What was God's presence like? How did you feel?

3. In what ways is your approach evocative? Describe a few evocative experiences.

4. Do you become didactic at times in supervision? Do you know what moves you into a didactic approach?

For Spiritual Directors

1. How does the looking into the well analogy relate to your experience of supervision? In what ways is your supervision experience contemplative and evocative? Give examples.

2. Can you identify with any of the four examples that have been described? In what way(s)?

3. What are some of the specific results you have experienced when your supervisor is contemplative and evocative?

4. What can help you be more aware while directing? Write a prayer asking God for the grace of inner awareness and the gift of a discerning heart.

A Contemplative Moment

Be with Jesus at the well. Together look into the well of your interior space. Dip the bucket into the well, and draw out one direction experience.

Feel the sparkling water of a contemplative atmosphere, clear insights, and a caring presence with the directee. Notice, too, the polluted areas of resistance, frustration, and failure.

With Jesus, hold both the darkness and the light, the struggles and the joys in your hands, and let the full experience reveal itself to you. Allow a growing awareness of reactions and reasons to emerge from this experience.

Savor the vibrant inner freedom that results from your contemplative awareness. Ask Jesus for the gifts of attentiveness so that you can be fully present with this person and with others.

Prayer for Inner Awareness

God of the well, thank you for inviting me to be with you at the well, my well. Thank you for always having time to be with me as I look into the the well of my interior life.

I am grateful for the opportunity to contemplate, explore, and savor the many rich experiences of spiritual direction that reside within that well. Thank you for your willingness to dip into my inner space and for your patience as we gently draw out an experience.

As we look together at pure areas of light and polluted areas of inner darkness, I ask you for the grace of inner awareness—an awareness that can look beneath the surface realities to deeper issues; an awareness that can unfold the various nuances and hidden dimensions of a painful experience and resulting vulnerability; an awareness that explores with patience and persistence; an awareness that leads to inner freedom and results in an open space for others.

You are a God of constant attentiveness. As my own limited awareness unfolds in the arena of your never-ending knowledge, give me the grace of a broader and deeper awareness of myself, of you, and of others.

Bathe my growing self-knowledge in the life-giving waters of your loving presence and healing touch.

4

Concretizing the Process:
The Skills of Supervision

As the spiritual director, supervisor, and God contemplatively gaze into the well of the director's interior life of direction experiences, deeper reactions and insights arise to the director's awareness. Specific supervision skills are needed to facilitate this self-awareness. Chapter 4 discusses four of these skills: listening, exploring, practical applications and role-playing, and feedback. It also describes three time frames that may be used for individual supervision.

Listening

Supervisors must be attentive to the interior life of the spiritual director and to the director's reactions in a verbatim case study (see learning experiences 5 and 6 for examples of verbatim case studies). They help directors to create the interior space that allows feelings to emerge gently and reverently. Supervisors also must create the space within themselves to be able to receive directors' experiences. They need to be attentive to the variety of interior movements that could occur within a director during a complete period, which includes the direction session itself, reflection time, verbatim preparation, and the current supervision session. This active and open listening results in awareness and clarification. The following guidelines can help supervisors to listen with discernment.

1. Prayerful reading of the verbatim case study

    a) Read the verbatim with an open heart and mind.

    b) Notice your own interior reactions while reading.

    Of the director's reactions that appear in the left column of the verbatim, what seems to be the strongest reaction? the strongest area of resistance? the place of greatest harmony with the directee?

    To what are you drawn to help the director explore?

    c) Take particular note of the director's verbal responses that are incongruent with the directee's experience.

    Which of the director's verbal responses seem to be dissonant with the directee's experience; that is, which responses move the directee away from his or her experience?

    d) Consider the reason the director brings a particular direction situation to supervision (see learning experience 3). Be sure the reason is discussed during the session as well as other dissonant areas in the verbatim case study.

2. Contemplative listening

    a) Listen to the director in an accepting, empathetic, and caring way.

    b) Listen prayerfully—that is, with conscious awareness of God's presence in the supervision session, in the director, and in oneself.

3. Revelatory listening

    a) Allow the director's inner experience to unfold in its own way and at its own pace. Let the interior experience reveal itself.

b) Have an open-ended rather than a predetermined stance. Remember that the supervisor does not control the unfolding of the director's inner life. He or she merely guides and brings it into focus.

c) Strive to maintain a reverent rather than a confrontative attitude of heart.

4. Evocative listening

a) Underscore key words. This (1) helps the directors feel that they have been heard, and (2) it encourages them to say more about their inner experience.

b) Paraphrase the affective experience—the key interior movements—of the director.

5. Focused listening

a) Notice particular reactions or issues that you sense would be important for the director to explore.

b) Focus on these reactions and issues as the supervision session proceeds.

c) Be present with the director in a felt way, letting yourself have an affective sense of what the director shares.

Exploring

The *process* of supervision is as important as the *product* of supervision. As much power exists in the exploratory process as in the insights that emerge from the exploration. Therefore, the supervisor needs to adopt a discovery approach. The supervisor underscores, paraphrases, asks questions, and reverently delves into what is happening within the director during a given direction session and the current supervision session. The supervisor focuses on specific reactions and feelings, unresolved issues and areas of unfreedom, and the subsequent insights that occur throughout supervision. This exploration leads to an experiential understanding of oneself as a spiritual director and as a person.

1. Unpack feelings.

    a) Invite the director to discuss a particular reaction in-depth.

        • "I notice that word 'repulsed' appears in the verbatim. Can you say more about your repulsed feeling?"

    b) Help the director recognize specific feelings.

        • "Tell me about your guilty feeling when Jim said that he couldn't 'get into' the suggestions for prayer that you recommended."

    c) Ask questions regarding the director's reactions during the supervision session.

        • "You're noticing now as we're talking that you felt helpless. Can you say more about that?"

        • "You are realizing now that you felt inadequate when your directee shared a story about his addiction to food. Would you like to say more about your feeling of inadequacy?"

2. Focus on concrete moments and particular experiences.

    a) Stay with a particular moment of the direction session where the director feels the strongest resistance.

        • "It was when Jean talked about God holding her that you felt the strongest movement away from her experience. Can you say what happened in you at that moment?"

    b) Help the director focus on painful life experiences that are only now coming into awareness.

- "So Jane's struggle with her father's fatal illness reminds you of the pain around your own mother's death. Would you like to talk about that?"

3. Explore unresolved issues and blind spots.

   a) Help the director become aware of unconscious or subconscious thoughts and feelings.

   - "You're noticing now your own fear of anger because of your parents' explosive expression of anger. Would you like to say more about that?"

   b) Help the director focus on blind spots that are beginning to reveal themselves.

   - "You're becoming aware of your desire to control Henry's tendency to feel sorry for himself. Can you say more about your desire to control that tendency?"

4. Savor and respond to religious experiences.

   a) Assist the director in listening more fully to and savoring more deeply the directee's experience of God.

   - "How do you feel about how you stayed with this directee's powerful experience of God? Is there any aspect of the experience that you could have lingered with longer? Do you have any sense of what was happening in you that prevented you from exploring deeper?"

   - "You struggled to help Tom go deeper into his experience when he mentioned that Jesus had his arm around his shoulder. Do you have a sense of what your struggle was about?"

   b) Help the director to be attentive to his or her own interior reactions to the directees' experiences of God.

- "You felt joyful when Joan sensed that God was embracing her. Can you say more about your joy?"

- "You felt envy when Tess sensed that God was crying with her. Do you know what caused this envy?"

c) Encourage the director to notice God's felt presence during direction sessions.

- "How would you describe God's presence during the session?"

- "At what point did you sense God's presence the strongest? What was God's presence like then?"

- "You sensed God as a caring companion with you as Jean shared her pain. Let's take a little time to savor God's caring stance because the more specifically you notice God's affective and concrete presence in one direction session, the more keenly you will be attuned to God's presence in other direction sessions."

d) Help the director notice God's felt absence during a given session and the reasons God seemed not to be affectively present.

- "You lost sight of God during this direction session. Let's look at that more closely so you can discover the reasons."

- "Direction sessions with this person seem to be too much like therapy, with little focus on God's presence. Let's look at what's happening because being aware of your own inner stance and approach will enable you to help this person focus more directly on God and the development of her prayer life."

5. Notice differences in one's affectivity and body.

    a) Assist the director in noticing the differences in his or her feelings that take place because of the sharing process.

        •   "Having felt and explored your fear of John's anger, how do you feel now?"

        •   "What differences do you notice in your interior space having felt and shared these various feelings and having noticed the reasons underneath them?"

    b) Invite the director to become aware of affective differences in his or her body.

        •   "How has your affectivity shifted since the beginning of this session? Feel the shift in your body and ponder the change within yourself."

        •   "As you notice these differences in your affectivity, can you also notice how and where these changes feel in your body? Take a moment of quiet now to experience these differences in your body."

6. Name felt insights and gather the graces.

    a) Allow insights to emerge emotionally and then intellectually, that is, from the gut to the heart to the head.

        •   "Having become aware of your feelings and changes in your feelings, what insights have you gained about yourself as a director? as a person? What have you learned about your directee? What have you learned about God's movement in people? in spiritual direction? in supervision?"

    b) Invite the director to gather the graces from the direction and supervision sessions.

- "How have you grown in your understanding of the spiritual direction process through this challenging direction session and our work today? How would you name the graces from this session?"

Practical Applications and Role-Playing

Having explored in-depth a particular issue and/or counter-movement and having lingered with God's felt presence or absence, supervisors can now help directors to envision concretely how they may respond differently to a directee in similar situations. That is, they can apply in a practical way the specific insights gained from supervision. Directors may simply articulate the different response, or they may choose to role-play, as if they were with a directee. Role-playing is used to allow these practical applications to come to life. The director and the supervisor also may role-play certain sections of the verbatim or direction session to help the director feel the directee's experience more keenly. The skill of making practical applications and the use of role-playing enables new awarenesses to emerge and fosters concrete learnings for future direction sessions. The following are some examples of practical applications and role-playing.

1. Make specific applications from new awarenesses.

   a) Deepen the director's awareness of where, how, and why (experiential reason) he or she moved away from the directee's experience and how a different response could have been made.

      - "Having explored your fear of intimacy and discovered the reason for it, let's read this section of the verbatim aloud so you can get a feel for how and where you left the directee's experience and how you would have rather responded."

   b) Explore ways in which the director may respond differently.

- "Now that you see that you moved away from Bern's experience of God embracing her because of your own fear of intimacy, how might you respond now to her experience? Let's role-play it. I'll be Bern, and you be yourself as her director."

c) Invite the spiritual director to find ways to remain aware of God's presence and to practice keeping a God-centered focus.

- "Having seen the underlying reason (being too controlling) for losing sight of God's presence during this direction session, let's look at what you might do next time in a similar situation to help yourself remain aware of God's presence."

- "Having seen what happens in you when you feel like you are doing therapy with this directee and having seen the reasons the sessions have not been focused on God, let's explore some ways you can help this person focus more directly on God." (The supervisor encourages the director to identify alternative ways to help the directee, offering suggestions only after the director exhausts all possibilities.) "Let's role-play a few of these ways."

2. Practice staying with a directee's experience.

   a) Practice exploring a directee's countermovement.

   - "Realizing how fearful you were of Donna's struggle and how and why you moved away from her darkness, how might you help her delve into her darkness now? Let's role-play it. I'll be Donna, and you be yourself as her director. Then afterward we can reflect on this role-playing."

   - "Seeing how and why (fear of a similar issue within oneself) you got caught up in Steve's rationalization and avoidance of the real issue, how might you go about this session differently? Let's role-play it. I'll be Steve, and you be yourself as his director."

b) Experience savoring a directee's explicit experience of God.

- "Seeing how and why (feelings of inadequacy) you avoided God's presence in Brad's very powerful experience of God, would you like to role-play this part, helping Brad to focus more directly on God's presence?"

3. Recognize your own interior movements and try to empathize with the directee's experience.

a) Read all or part of the verbatim aloud, with the director role-playing the directee and you role-playing the director.

- "To get a feel for Bern's intimate experience of God, let's read aloud this section of the verbatim. Why don't you be Bern, and I'll be you."

b) Read all or part of the verbatim aloud, with the director as him- or herself. You can be the directee.

- "To get in touch with the felt reactions you were having during this session, let's read the verbatim aloud. I'll be the directee, and you can be yourself."

Feedback

After the first three skills of supervision have been used as fully as possible, the supervisor offers constructive feedback at the end of the session to facilitate further reflection and exploration by the director. This feedback helps the director's ongoing growth as a person and as a spiritual director, and it fosters the integration of insights.

1. Summarize movements and insights. Underscore three or four significant ones that have emerged through the exploratory process. Be specific and concrete.

   • "You have become aware that you still have some unresolved issues and hurt feelings regarding your parents' explosive anger that has prevented you from allowing your directee to express her anger."

   • "Through this session the source of your fear of intimacy (identify it) is clearer to you, as is the realization that this fear can prevent you from staying with directees' intimate experiences of God."

2. Acknowledge affective differences, and name areas of growing freedom.

   a) Acknowledge affective differences.

   • "You are not feeling burdened by the directee's seeming lack of progress as you were when we started out today. You're more lighthearted."

   • "You are feeling less fearful, freer to be with Tom in his intense grief now that you have acknowledged your own deep feelings over the loss of your mother."

   b) Name some areas of growing insight and freedom.

   • "Through noticing the reason for your agitation—your own incomplete grieving over your mother's death—you seem to be more able and desirous to let Jane express her grief."

- "You feel more open to going to an ACOA (Adult Children of Alcoholics) meeting as a result of our session today."

3. Suggest questions and areas for further reflection and prayer.

   - "Even though you became aware of a lot today during our time together (name the areas of awarenesses), I would encourage you to spend some time in God's presence reflecting about your tendency to control. See what else surfaces, and jot your reflections down."

   - "You may want to the ponder the question: 'What are some other experiences that have made me fearful of anger?'"

4. Underscore growing edges.

   - "Notice again in this verbatim how you distanced yourself from your directee's intense feelings when she cried—how uncomfortable you were with strong feelings."

   - "Even though you have grown in your ability to stay with directees' intimate experiences of God, notice the subtle way you moved away from Bern's intimate experience of God. It's an area in which you need to do more work."

5. Affirm ways in which the director is growing personally and professionally.

   - "You are gaining concrete awarenesses of interior movements in yourself and in your directees. You are much more self-aware than you were six months or so ago."

   - "You are more keenly aware of the Spirit moving in yourself and in your directees."

- "You really helped Tom get in touch with his anger at God."

- "You are really growing in your ability to help Bill explore his shame surrounding his addiction and bring the shame to God in prayer."

Time Frames for Individual Supervision Sessions

Three time frames for an individual session can be used: (1) a one-hour session; (2) a one-and-one-half hour session; and (3) a two-hour session. The time frame is determined by how often supervision will occur and the duration of a training program. For instance, a one-year training program that meets weekly usually has a one-hour time frame for individual supervision. A two- or three-year program with individual supervision every other week often requires a longer duration. The following is a suggested format for individual supervision, structured in relation to the time frame and the use of skills.

One-Hour Supervision Session

1. Supervisor's reading of verbatim	15 minutes
2. Listening and exploration	30 minutes
3. Practical application/role-playing	10 minutes
4. Feedback	5 minutes

One-and-One-Half-Hour Supervision Session

1. Supervisor's reading of verbatim	15 minutes
2. Listening and exploration	50 minutes
3. Practical application/role-playing	15 minutes
4. Feedback	10 minutes

Two-Hour Supervision Session

1. Supervisor's reading of verbatim   15 minutes

2. Listening and exploration   75 minutes

3. Practical application/role-playing   20 minutes

4. Feedback   10 minutes

Conclusion

Supervision helps spiritual directors become aware of various movements while in the process of directing, and it allows them to grow in interior freedom in order to stay in tune with their directees' life and God experiences. Through the process and skills of supervision, supervisors attempt to assist directors in three ways: (1) to recognize when, how, and why they move away from directees's experiences, to avoid doing so in future sessions; (2) to notice more specifically and savor more deeply their directees' explicit experiences of God; and (3) to apply insights that emerged during supervision toward future direction sessions. The four supervision skills of listening, exploring, practical application and role-playing, and feedback assist directors' growing self-knowledge, develop an awareness of experiential insights and inner freedom, and enhance the capacity to linger longer with their directees' experiences.

Questions for Reflection and Discussion

For Supervisors

1. In what specific ways do you use a verbatim case study during supervision sessions? Give examples.

2. Other springboards or tools that can be used during supervision are (*a*) director writes a process paper; (*b*) director writes an overall description of direction situation; or (*c*) director gives an oral overview of a direction experience. Have you used any of these approaches? What are the advantages and disadvantages of each?

3. What supervision skills do you use most? What advantages and disadvantages have you discovered with each of the four skills?

4. What are some ways that you have used the skill of role-playing during supervision? Give examples.

5. Give some examples of blind spots that have arisen during supervision that hamper directors' awareness. Can you describe concretely one incident of this dynamic?

6. What are specific ways that you help the director make practical applications to a direction session after exploring in-depth?

7. What time frame for supervision have you found most helpful? Why?

For Spiritual Directors

1. What do you find helpful about using a verbatim case study for supervision? unhelpful?

2. What advantages and disadvantages have you experienced through the use of each of the four supervision skills: listening, exploration, practical applications and role-playing, and feedback?

3. Which supervision skills have been especially useful in your experience?

4. What blind spots and new insights have emerged through the skill of exploration? How did you change as a result of becoming aware?

5. What aspects of supervision are most challenging for you? most beneficial? most rewarding?

6. What time frame for individual supervision have you found most helpful? Why?

A Contemplative Moment

Sit with each of your directees and/or your supervisees, and let the living waters of God's loving presence flow over each one. Contemplate the brokenness and vulnerability they have shared with you. See the living waters of God's healing light seep into their woundedness. Ask God for the courage to be with them in their broken places.

Sit with yourself in the same manner, and ask God for the strength to let the living waters of God's gentleness permeate your weakness, fears, and vulnerability.

Prayer for Courage and Strength

God of courage, as I enter into my own brokenness and that of others, help me to do so with courage and strength. Give me the confidence to know that with you all things are possible, even the intimate and vulnerable experience of delving into darkness and pain.

As the living waters of your love permeate my being, I ask for the strength to face the polluted realities that emerge from within me.

As those in my care delve into their areas of unfreedom and strive to discover your presence, give me the courage to enter into their darkness with them and to guide them to the light of your love.

| 5 |

Exemplifying the Purposes, Content, Process, and Skills: Three Case Studies

Case studies effectively illustrate the dynamics of supervision, demonstrating the spiritual director and supervisor drawing water from the well of the director's interior experiences. This chapter uses three case studies to exemplify the purposes, content, process, and skills of supervision. The first case study illustrates a struggle with a vulnerable personal issue. The second study exemplifies a mirroring dynamic. The third study describes a breakthrough in learning the principles of contemplative spiritual direction. I invite you to imagine each spiritual director, each supervisor, and Jesus sitting at the well reverently contemplating the director's interior experience.

Case Study 1: Joe's Struggle with Intimacy

Spiritual Direction Session

Joe, a Catholic priest, has been involved in spiritual direction for four years. He is directing Doris.

Background of Directee

Doris has had a close personal relationship with God for many years. In this direction session Doris shares an intimate experience that occurred as she shared with Jesus her anger and hurt over not being accepted in a ministry position that she really wanted and felt she deserved.

Excerpt from a Verbatim Case Study

Director's Reactions	Conversation
	Doris 1: I shared with God how hurt I was because I wasn't accepted for the job when I was led to believe I would be. I could feel God's presence as I shared and cried some more.
	Joe 1: You could feel God's presence.
Discomfort	D2: Yes, Jesus was right there listening to me. Then all of a sudden I noticed he was crying too.
	J2: Jesus was crying too?
	D3: Yes, he was crying for me.
Anxiety	J3: He was crying for you. Can you say more?
Too much for me!	D4: Yes, he was with me in my pain. He was feeling the same hurt I was feeling. He felt my humiliation.
Envy	J4: He was feeling your pain and humiliation.
	D5: Yes, he felt how humiliated and rejected I felt.
	J5: How did you feel when you sensed Jesus so close to you, sharing the pain and rejection you were feeling?
	D6: I felt so loved by him, so one with him. I felt some hope that I might get over this because he was so close to me in my pain.

Reason for Bringing This Experience to Supervision

Joe has been struggling with issues related to intimacy. He has a difficult time getting in touch with his deeper feelings and communicating authentically with others and God. He brings this verbatim to supervision because of his strong negative reactions to Doris' intimate experience and because of his emotional distancing during the direction session.

Supervison Purposes, Process, and Skills

Supervision Session with Mary

Mary 1: Joe, you have the word "discomfort" written next to Doris's statement: ". . . I noticed he was crying too." Can you say more about your uncomfortable feeling?

Joe 1: Well, it kind of startled me when she said that. And then I had the feeling, "Oh no."

M2: You had an "oh no" feeling.

J2: Yeah, it was a feeling like "Let me get out of here!"

M3: Can you say more about what you felt when you said to yourself, "Let me get out of here!"?

J3: This was too close for comfort for me. Then, as I said later in the verbatim, I felt envy.

M4: You felt envy.

J4: Yes. Doris has such a close relationship with Jesus, and I'd like a closer relationship with him, but I'm afraid.

M5: You're afraid?

J5: I'm afraid of what he might ask of me if I get too close. I don't mean work-type things. I mean I'm afraid he might want me to be vulnerable.

M6:   He might want you to be vulnerable.

J6:   Yes, and if I'm vulnerable with him or with anyone I might lose control. Underneath this "cool, together" facade are a lot of strong feelings. As we talk now I'm realizing I'm afraid of the strength of my feelings. If I really start sharing them with God or another person, they might overwhelm me. I saw that too often between my parents. My mother would express one little feeling to my father and before you knew it they would get into a big fight. When my father wouldn't respond to her, she would go bananas. I would have to leave the room because I couldn't stand it. I'm just making this connection now. I've only seen negative results from sharing your feelings. No wonder I have such a hard time expressing my feelings to God or anyone else.

      (Mary spends a significant amount of time helping Joe to explore this concrete experience in-depth.)

M7:   (Later) Joe, what you're describing about your parents sounds so hard. How do you feel sharing all that?

J7:   I'm feeling really mad now at my parents. No wonder I have such a hard time feeling my feelings. (Mary helps Joe to express his feelings and then invites him to share with God his anger and fear of being vulnerable. She also helps Joe notice how his lack of awareness led him to distance himself from Doris. Eventually they return to the direction session and the verbatim.)

M8:   Joe, having seen the connection between your reactions to Doris's intimate experience of Jesus and your fear of intense feelings, how do you feel now about Doris's experience and being with her in the next session?

J8:   I feel so much lighter now, freer. I feel like I can be more fully present to Doris. (Pause) In fact I feel more of a joy for Doris rather than feeling envy or wanting to run away. Her experience of Jesus is really touching.

(Mary helps Joe savor the new inner freedom he is experiencing now and encourages him to spend time in prayer before meeting with Doris again in spiritual direction.)

Process: Three "R's" of Supervision

Reactions	Reasons	Results
Discomfort	With intimacy.	Self-awareness. Self-knowledge.
Envy	Of Doris's close relationship,	"
Fear	of being vulnerable,	"
	of losing control,	"
	of strong feelings. Concrete reason is an unresolved issue:	
	parents' fighting;	"
	out-of-control expression of feelings.	Hidden reality brought into the light.
	Final result: interior freedom; greater ability to stay with directees' experiences.	

Supervision Purposes and Skills

By contemplatively looking into the well of a direction experience, Joe connects his strong distancing reactions to a painful childhood experience. Mary stays with the connection and helps Joe bring dark memories into the light. She listens to his experience in a caring and gentle way, persistently encouraging him to explore his childhood memories by expressing his feelings about them. She helps him realize how his attitude toward Doris changed and offers concrete suggestions for prayer before he meets with her again.

Case Study 2: Joan's Growing Awareness of Codependent Issues

Supervision on Directed Retreats

While offering directed retreats, spiritual directors often do not have the time to draft a written verbatim for supervision. Therefore they take notes on each of their directees and their own reactions, using a spiritual direction log. Like ongoing spiritual direction, the main focus of supervision is on the interior movements of the director. Spiritual directors with less experience in giving directed retreats, however, may also be given practical aids and suggestions, such as the use of Scripture.

Background

Joan is a talented forty-three-year-old director of religious education in a vibrant parish. An experienced spiritual director, she offers directed retreats under supervision for further growth. In this particular case study she is directing four people on a weekend retreat. Marge is her supervisor.

Day 1: An Excerpt from the Conversation

Joan 1: Several of my retreatants talked very openly about the effects of their parents' alcoholism on themselves and resulting codependent issues. I was present with them as they shared their prayer. But when they talked about the codependent and alcoholic issues, I felt an emotional distancing within myself.

Marge 1: You felt an emotional distancing within yourself?

J2:   Yes it was subtle, but it was there. It became even clearer as I reflected on it later and took notes.

When they shared information about their issues, I distanced myself.

M2: Was there a particular issue or retreatant with whom you felt the emotional distancing to be stronger than with the others? (Marge helps her to be concrete.)

J3: Yes, one of them mentioned that she is dealing with her strong tendency to be too responsible for others and therefore neglecting her own needs. She also discussed the difficulty she has trusting people in a deep way. These two issues struck me because I have been noticing these in myself the past several months.

M3: You're noticing your tendency to be too responsible and to neglect your own needs along with your struggle to trust.

J4: Yes. My mother was an alcoholic, which I've known for years. But it's only in the past six months that I'm realizing the impact of her alcoholism on me. I'm feeling a lot of loneliness lately, and I'm realizing it is because I'm so busy doing for others that I don't take care of my own friendship needs. I'm realizing, too, that I have trouble being vulnerable even with my closest friends. I act like I have it together when I'm hurting inside.

M4: So you feel lonely at times and have a hard time being vulnerable even with your closest friends.

J5: Yes, I feel so alone sometimes. I tend to process things within myself, and I might tell my friends about the struggle later after it's over. I get to a point of inner crisis and feel such intense feelings that I feel like I could explode. And I keep it all to myself. Then when the crisis is all over I forget about it and get back into working hard and forgetting about myself and my needs. I've got to stop doing that.

(Later) I'm feeling a need to talk to a counselor who is aware of codependent issues, and I've also thought about going to a Codependents Anonymous meeting. I want to stop overlooking myself and my needs. I need to do more things for me. (As the conversation continued, Joan realized her fear of focusing on herself too much and her fear of becoming selfish and self-centered if she spends a significant amount of time talking about herself.)

M5: (Later in the session) Having explored these specific issues today (Marge identifies them) and your feelings related to these (identifies the feelings), how do you feel being with your retreatants tomorrow?

J6:   I'm happy that I became aware of so much today. I want to spend time in prayer with this. Something I have kept so private I have finally got out in the open with you. I feel less burdened. I am in a much better space to listen to my retreatants. I can be more present to them and to God during the sessions.

Day 2

Joan 1: I felt different today with my retreatants. I felt more emotionally connected. I could feel their pain. I could feel a sense of identification with their issues rather than wanting to run away emotionally.

Marge 1: I'm happy for you that you felt emotionally connected with your retreatants. Can you share an instance of this?

J2:   Yes, I could feel the frustration of one person who has a very responsible job and who is trying to deal with herself and her own needs. I could feel her struggle and discouragement. It's very similar to my struggle. (They stay with this for a while.)

M2: Joan, could you say more about feeling emotionally connected with your retreatants? what that connection felt like in you?

J3:   It felt like my whole self was there. Yesterday I felt like only part of me was there. I felt a wholeness within myself today. (Pause) I didn't realize that until you asked that question.

M3: You felt a wholeness within yourself, like your whole self was there.

J4: Yes, I felt freer within myself, more present. I felt like I was fully there. I felt the pain of my retreatants, like I was really with them. I felt a deep sense of really being myself with them.

M4: Is there a particular moment or moments where you felt a sense of wholeness and of being yourself? (Joan discusses two such moments and the joy that she felt when she realized that the emotional distance was no longer there and that she was fully present.)

(Later in session)

M5: What would you say was the grace(s) of this retreat for you, Joan?

J5: (Reflects for a moment) I feel a deep movement to do something about tending to my own needs, to process things, and to be more vulnerable. I'm going to make an appointment with an alcohol counselor. And I'm going to go to an ACOA meeting or to Codependents Anonymous. I feel a deep invitation from God to do something about this. I've been putting it off for too long. I truly can feel God drawing me to these two concrete actions. (They spend time contemplating God's invitation as God draws Joan to a deeper connection with herself.)

M6: How does that feel, experiencing that drawing from God?

J6: I feel an excitement about it. It feels so right to do this for me. I've got to stop thinking about going to those meetings and just go. I feel a drawing from God to take care of myself and to grow in greater wholeness.

Supervision Purposes, Process, and Skills

Day 1: Noticing and Unpacking Resistance

In the actual supervision experience, the purposes, process, and skills are unfolding congruently and simultaneously. This unfolding is described below.

1. Begin with an *initial, more noticeable reaction:* emotional distancing.

    a) The director brings up the point of focus.

    b) Usually deeper feelings and unresolved issues lie underneath, such as detachment, boredom, distraction, frustration.

2. Focus on a *particular moment* when that reaction was *strongest;* that is, when the retreatant shared the issue of being too responsible and not vulnerable enough.

    a) The director can get in touch with the feeling again, which enables the unfolding to go deeper.

    b) Focusing helps to keep the director rooted in an affective way rather than reflecting in a heady way.

    c) By talking about a specific moment, underlying feelings and issues come out into the open. What is hidden comes out into the light.

3. Explore *reasons underneath reactions,* such as unresolved issues of overresponsiblity and self-neglect.

    a) Brings into the light deeper areas of unfreedom.

    b) The power of these hidden areas is dissipated through awareness and sharing with another.

    c) Interior freedom grows in the director.

4. *Continue to explore.* Joan talks about her loneliness, of not taking care of her own needs, of her need for change, of her fear of becoming too focused on self.

   a) The more directors notice and understand their underlying feelings and issues, the freer they become.

5. *Make applications to direction sessions.* Marge helps Joan focus on how she feels about being with her directees.

   a) Notice differences in oneself by exploring inner realities in-depth with someone.

   b) Enables directors to be more present with directees and to savor their experiences more deeply.

Day 2: Noticing and Savoring Resulting Freedom

By unpacking the feelings and unresolved issues underneath the emotional distancing, Joan has become freer and more able to be present with her retreatants in a contemplative way.

1. Focus on *difference:* emotional connection.

   a) Directors can feel new freedom and growth.

   b) Directors can be more present with directees from a place of consonance and freedom rather than from dissonance and resistance.

2. Assist the *unfolding of the initial response:* notice the sense of wholeness, inner freedom, and empathy.

   a) Feeling and savoring newly found interior freedom enables this freedom to continue to be strengthened in future direction sessions.

3. Facilitate the noticing and savoring of *particular moments of freedom:* awareness of excitement and joy.

    a) Directors' inner freedom grows more alive and real.

    b) Directors experience the consolation more deeply and can feel excitement about it.

4. Focus on *God's presence*: Joan feels drawn to concrete action.

    a) God is active in spiritual directors' experiences.

    b) Focusing specifically on God enables spiritual directors to notice God's presence and invitation.

Case Study 3: Tony's Breakthrough as a Spiritual Director

Beginning spiritual directors, especially those in the early years of a training program, often need to develop a contemplative and evocative approach to spiritual direction. In addition to becoming aware of inner realities and areas of darkness, as illustrated by Joe's and Joan's experience, they also need to notice when they are being heady or didactic and when they are acting as problem solvers and advice givers during direction sessions. Although experienced spiritual directors can also have these tendencies, they are more likely to catch themselves and change their approach to a more contemplative and evocative one. Through courses, workshops, and supervision, directors can develop a discerning heart, a prayerful presence, and a contemplative approach to spiritual direction. By focusing on the ability to help directees savor their experiences of God, supervision assists beginning directors in savoring religious experience and exploring life experience. The following situation describes a beginning spiritual director who changes his approach to spiritual direction as a result of supervision.

Background

Tony, an ordained minister for more than twenty years, is in the first year of a three-year training program for spiritual directors. Tony needs to address four issues: (1) to focus more directly on experiences of God rather than taking a problem-solving approach; (2) to help directees to savor their experiences of God rather than only identify them; (3) to be less controlling and more open to directees' unfolding inner process; and (4) to focus on affectivity and to ask "feeling" questions rather than focusing on thoughts and asking "thinking" questions. The following supervision session with Barbara describes a powerful breakthrough for Tony in his approach to spiritual direction.

Tony 1: During the last several supervision sessions, you have been helping me to see how easily I can fall into a problem-solving and teaching mode. I'm seeing that I talk too much, especially when I don't know where to go next with a directee. And when I feel nervous, I can control the session.

   I'm bringing this verbatim today because something very exciting happened in me during the session. A lightbulb finally went on in my head and heart. I feel like I'm finally getting it.

Barbara 1: Gosh, that's great, Tony. Let's talk about what happened in you and what you learned during this direction session.

T2: I was really looking forward to coming today. It's like new lights went on in me during this session. It was so powerful. I can feel such a difference in me during direction sessions since then.

B2: That's wonderful! (Pause) Let's take our time and look at precisely what happened in you and why. Where in the verbatim did the lightbulb start going on?

T3: It was at my third response when I said to my directee, "Kate, let me see the Bible (closing it). We're not here to pull meaning out of Scripture. We're here to see how God is working in your life. Have you had any sense of God with you this week?" You see, I'm the one who was giving her scripture passages to pray with each week, and that wasn't going anywhere. Kate was trying to figure out meanings. The direction sessions have been dry and dis-connected. The sessions were becoming heady, as you challenged me to see during our last supervision session with another directee.

B3:   And what happened in you after you said that to Kate?

T4:   The whole session changed. Kate started talking about the strained relationship she has had with her sister and how God was with her when she finally visited her sister. For a change I focused more on her feelings than her thoughts. You challenged me about that tendency of mine a few sessions ago.

B4:   Yes, I remember that! And describe what happened in you as you changed your approach.

T5:   I finally stopped trying to control the sessions and Kate's prayer. I let her talk about her experience with her sister and how God was close to her then. Kate came alive, I came alive, and the whole session changed. It was so powerful, so foundational for me as a spiritual director. I'm finally getting it!

B5:   Tell me about your coming alive and the power you felt.

T6:   I had a strong feeling of relief when I closed the Bible. Closing the Bible was symbolic of my letting go of the control. And when I let go and stopped controlling the session, new life poured into me. There was a new vitality in me. It was so overwhelming.

B6:   Yes, you let her talk about the Scripture of her life, and then both you and Kate came alive.

T7:   Yes, exactly. That's a good way of saying it. When I stopped "making" her meditate on the Scriptures and let her talk about the Scripture of her life, the whole session changed. I changed. It's like I put on a new pair of glasses. I finally saw, from my heart, how I needed to be with her. I listened to her experience with her sister and helped her talk about her feelings and how God was with her. I stopped being a clinician and started being a companion. I listened to everything Kate said instead of narrowly focusing on one thing and missing a lot of other things. I was focusing only on the meditations I encouraged her to do each week and was missing who she really is and how God is present with her and in her. The whole experience was so exciting.

B7: Yes, this truly is exciting. It's like all the hard work we have been doing during supervision is finally bearing fruit. (Both laugh.) How did you feel, Tony, when you finally let go of the control and listened from your heart to Kate's whole story?

T8: I felt so grateful to God that I was finally getting it. It was such a joy to be with Kate and to help her notice God. Doing spiritual direction was feeling like such a chore lately but that feeling changed—I felt such an enthusiasm, a vitality growing in me. (Pause) I also felt a deep confidence as a director, a deep sense of confirmation about myself as a spiritual director. This session was such a gift.

B8: Yes, it certainly sounds like it. So you felt joy, vitality, enthusiasm, growing confidence, and sense of confirmation as a director. Did you sense God's presence there with yourself and Kate?

T9: Yes, I did. (Pauses and reflects) I felt God very present with us, but I'm just realizing now as you ask me about God that God was present as a physician, the Divine Physician, helping Kate's wound and her strained relationship with her sister open up and allow all the poison to come out. I was like God's helper, like an assisting physician.

B9: God was the Divine Physician, and you were an assisting physician in opening up Kate's wound. That's a beautiful analogy. Can you say more about God as a Divine Physician with Kate? Then we will look at your stance there.

T10: (Pauses, and then slowly and thoughtfully) God was very tender with Kate, caring and loving. God was so tenderly present with Kate in helping her keep this deep wound. God wanted Kate's pain and anger to pour out because she has kept it inside herself for so long. (Barbara continues to help Tony savor God's tender, loving, and caring presence.)

B10: That's very touching, Tony. How did you feel seeing God as such a tender and caring Divine Physician?

T11: It was so sacred, so holy. I felt like I was on holy ground as Kate shared her pain. And I was not the main physician, God was. I was more like a wounded healer who was accepting and understanding Kate's wound. I was like a wounded companion walking with her rather than a clinician figuring it all out and telling her what she needed to do. What a difference inside of me!

B11: You were God's assistant and a wounded companion with Kate. That's a different stance for you. Say more about that difference inside of you.

T12: My heart was more open to Kate, because I was coming more from my heart than my head. I was present with her rather than working on her. Emotionally, I felt more connected. I was identifying with her from my own woundedness, again being more of a wounded healer. I let God be the head doctor, and I was both God's and Kate's companion. What a shift inside of me. It felt so great. (Barbara helps Tony notice more felt inner realities about being a wounded healer and companion. She helps him savor the shift occurring within him.) And I noticed such a big difference in myself during other direction sessions.

B12: So that deep shift inside you affected other direction sessions?

T13: Yes, I noticed I was truly listening with an open heart to everything my directees shared, rather than half listening and imposing my agenda on them. I let my suggestions for prayer flow from their experience rather than giving scripture passages that were not speaking to their hearts anyway. I'm noticing now that my desire to be a spiritual director is growing stronger. I continue to feel a deep confirmation from God. The experience with Kate was so foundational for me as a spiritual director. (Barbara continues to help Tony explore the differences he notices within himself and, concretely, how this was a foundational experience for him.)

B13: (At the end of the session) What has happened in you, Tony, is truly significant for you as a spiritual director. You are moving from seeing spiritual direction as a method and as a series of techniques to accepting basic principles about the spiritual direction process, such as staying with directees' agendas rather than imposing yours on them; listening from a deeper place inside of you rather than being attentive with your mind only. Also, you are more aware of God in your sessions; that you are God's co-worker and your directees' caring companion. (Barbara underscores other insights.) So many wonderful insights and learnings are jelling for you from this experience. Many seeds have been planted from other direction and supervision sessions, and now they are all starting to blossom. I feel very happy for you and excited to see the change in you. (Barbara also suggests concrete ways for Tony to stay with and to deepen his growing knowledge of basic principles concerning a contemplative approach to spiritual direction.)

Supervision Purposes, Process, and Skills

Barbara has been Tony's companion, walking with him on the journey of becoming a spiritual director. She listens from the heart and observes the surprising ways that God reveals Self. During this supervision session she helps Tony savor the richness of this graced experience, noticing God's presence as a tender and loving Divine Physician and recognizing his own presence as an assisting physician and wounded healer. In this new stance Tony realizes the difference between *doing* spiritual direction and *being* a spiritual director. He also experiences the difference between *technique*—doing the tasks of a spiritual director—and *presence,* being a God-centered and loving companion to his directees. He engages in the deeper mystery of being a spiritual director not only doing *for* God and others but also sharing *with* God and others. Barbara helps Tony to notice the differences in his approach and presence with other directees. She helps him to explore the many powerful insights that finally came together for him after hard work in previous supervision sessions, and she offers feedback for further reflection and growth.

Consoling experiences, such as Tony's direction session with Kate, are a gift for the supervisor as well as the directee. Together, in God's presence, they can celebrate the fruits of their many hours of hard work. They can let themselves be drenched in the refreshing waters of God's affective presence, transformative insights, growing freedom, and new life. Having explored the "pollution" of Tony's narrow and unfruitful approach to spiritual direction in previous supervision sessions, they can now enjoy the purity of the living waters of God's loving presence. What a marvelous blessing!

Conclusion

In a caring and contemplative way, Joe's, Joan's, and Tony's supervisors help them to look into the well of particular direction experiences, savor God's vibrant presence, and explore their interior movements. By an evocative and exploratory approach, the supervisors facilitate their awareness of deeper felt reactions and underlying reasons for these reactions. In this way the directors develop a greater self-awareness, which enables them to grow in deeper interior freedom. Because of their growing self-knowledge and freedom as persons and as spiritual directors, in future sessions they will be more fully present and better able to help their directees explore vulnerable personal issues and to savor their experiences of God in greater depth.

Questions for Reflection and Discussion

For Supervisors

1. What is most noticeable to you about the supervisors' approach and focus with Joe? with Joan? with Tony?

2. What particular supervision skills most apply in each of the sessions?

3. What learnings or insights about supervision did you gain or were reaffirmed by these case studies? What were your feelings as you read and pondered each?

4. What might you explore further with Joe? with Joan? with Tony? What feedback might you offer? Role-play your exploration and feedback with each.

5. Remember a supervision session during which you helped a director notice specific details about God's affective presence in a direction session. What was the director's experience of God like? How did that experience affect his or her way of "being" as a director? What happened in you as the director unfolded and savored this graced experience?

For Spiritual Directors

1. What is most noticeable to you about Joe's, Joan's, and Tony's direction experiences? supervision experiences?

2. Can you remember a direction session similar to Joe's; that is, when a directee's consoling experience triggered resistance around a vulnerable area? Relive that experience and process your reactions with someone or in writing. What were the reasons underlying your reactions? What new insights have you gained by processing it now?

3. Can you remember a direction experience like Joan's, when you were dealing with a similar issue as your directee's (mirroring dynamic)? Ponder that experience. What was the issue you were mirroring? What were your reactions when you were with your directee? Did you process your reactions in supervision? If so, what differences did you notice in yourself when you were with your directee?

4. Can you remember a supervision experience like Tony's, when you experienced and processed a powerful breakthrough as a spiritual director? Describe concretely your breakthrough. What was God's presence like? What new insights did you gain about spiritual direction and your approach as a spiritual director? How did you change as a spiritual director as a result of that breakthrough?

5. Reflect on the differences between *doing* spiritual direction and *being* a spiritual director. How would you describe the differences? In what specific ways have you experienced these differences in relation to your own ministry of spiritual direction?

6. Remember and relive a spiritual direction session when you experienced God in the unfolding of someone's experience of God. What was God's presence like? How did you feel? What difference did this experience make in your stance as a spiritual director?

A Contemplative Moment

Remember a recent session when you were with someone who was in deep pain. What was the person's pain like? How were you present to that person? How did you feel? Where was God in that experience?

Embrace that person's struggle now as you compassionately hold the pain. Ask God to be with you in this compassionate way in future sessions with this person and others.

Prayer for a Compassionate Heart

God of compassion, I ask for the gift of a compassionate heart, a heart that can enter into the pain of others and embrace it as my own. Let my heart be like the womb of Yahweh, holding others' suffering as new life is born in them.

Jesus, Incarnate One, transform my heart into a heart of flesh and blood like yours, a heart totally human that can bleed with others in their struggles and rejoice with them in their joy. As you dwelt among us, totally human in all things, give me a totally human heart to dwell with others in their human suffering, despair, hope, and joy.

I ask for the confidence to know that when my small heart is one with your compassionate heart, together we can embrace the many faces of human suffering that come our way.

$$\boxed{6}$$

A Shared Contemplative Experience: Peer Group Supervision of Spiritual Directors

---

A rich experience of supervision can occur in a group as well as individually. Peer group supervision takes place when three or more spiritual directors assemble and one or more directors present a direction situation for supervision. The same approach, process, and skills are used in individual supervision. However, the group usually follows a prescribed format. Chapter 6 describes two models of peer group supervision: (1) a structure and process for ongoing spiritual direction and (2) a structure and process used during retreats. It also discusses dynamics and atmosphere, the role of the facilitator, reminders, and advantages and disadvantages of peer group supervision. Learning experience 12 provides an outline of each model that can be used during peer group sessions.

Model 1: Peer Group Supervision for Ongoing Spiritual Direction

Spiritual directors often gather for peer group supervision regularly, usually monthly, while participating in a training program and for ongoing development. A director in a training program often presents a verbatim case study; however, an experienced spiritual director may present a written or oral overview of the direction situation without a verbatim. The format and components of model 1 as well as suggested time frames follow.

Format and Components

A.   *Presentation of case*: The director presents background and verbatim.

1.   The presenting director shares brief information about the directee, giving a copy of the verbatim to each member of the group. Strict confidentiality is maintained throughout.

2.   Two people read aloud the conversation from the written verbatim as the others read along or listen.

Reason: This reading animates the conversation, helps the group to become centered, and encourages getting in touch with their own feelings.

3.   The group takes several moments of quiet time to allow their minds, hearts, and spirits to absorb the direction experience and to gain a sense of God's guiding Spirit. They may circle on the verbatim "feeling" words and areas of needed focus.

4.   The group asks questions about the directee or the session that will help the exploration part of supervision.

5.   The presenting spiritual director shares

a) his or her feelings about the direction session.

b) his or her reasons for presenting this case, and particular areas on the verbatim that may need more attention.

c) an area of focus that might be helpful to explore.

B. *Group exploration:* A contemplative and evocative approach is taken.

1. Group exploration forms the core experience of supervision, out of which evolves feedback and insights. Most of the time is spent here.

2. Group helps the presenting spiritual director to

    a) unpack deeper feelings and explore the experiential reasons underlying the initial reactions stated in the left-hand column of the verbatim;

    b) discover additional feelings and insights surrounding an area of unfreedom, resistance, or struggle;

    c) savor God's felt presence and notice God's felt absence during a session; and

    d) create an inner space for feelings, issues, and areas of resistance to reveal themselves gently and reverently.

Reason for a contemplative approach: Allows for challenging and vulnerable inner areas to reveal themselves in a gentle and God-centered manner.

Reason for an evocative approach: Feelings have greater power and insights have deeper impact when individuals discover them on their own (with assistance from others) than when others do it for them.

C. *Group prayer and feedback:* Specific observations are shared.

1. Time is made for quiet prayer, to

    a) provide space for participants to be in touch with God in a more explicit way that relates to what the director disclosed during the exploratory part of the session;

    b) ask God for a discerning vision of heart to notice and identify a significant insight that can be shared with the presenting director;

    c) give the presenting director time to review his or her inner experience from beginning to end, paying particular attention to any differences or changes that may have occurred within one-self; and

    d) pray for the director in a specific way in relation to what was shared.

2.   Sharing of observations and insights:

Each person shares one observation, insight, image, feeling, suggestion, or question that can assist the presenting director's ongoing growth.

    a) It can be an insight or feeling that became clear during group exploration or something from their own experience of directing.

    b) It can be an image that surfaced during the supervision session or during quiet prayer.

    c) Presenter shares significant insights and feelings that came to consciousness as a result of this supervision session.

3.   Reasons for feedback:

    a) Gives the group an opportunity to underscore or share their most significant observations.

    b) Assists the presenting director with further insights into him- or herself and offers concrete suggestions for working with the directee or examining a particular issue.

4. Writing down feedback:
    A participant writes down feedback from each person to encourage the presenter's continued prayerful discernment after the group session has ended.

D. *Group learnings:* Key experiential insights are shared.

1. Each participant shares a significant insight about God, prayer, religious experience, life experience, spiritual growth, spiritual direction, or supervision that was learned or reinforced during the session. A supervision session can serve as an instrument of deeper experiential learning about any of these areas.

2. Optional (if knowledgeable of the *Spiritual Exercises*): Each participant may relate the spiritual direction or supervision experience to the Rules for Discernment or the Weeks of the *Spiritual Exercises.*

Suggested Time Frame

One-and-one-half-hour peer group session: Three or four people

A.	Presentation of case	15 minutes
B.	Group exploration	45 minutes
C.	Group prayer and feedback	15 minutes
D.	Group learnings	15 minutes

Two-hour peer group session: Four to six people

A.	Presentation of case	15 minutes
B.	Group exploration	60 minutes
C.	Group prayer and feedback	20 minutes

| Break | 10 minutes |
| D. Group learnings | 15 minutes |

Two-and-one-half-hour peer group session: Seven or more people

A. Presentation of case	15 minutes
B. Group exploration	70 minutes
C. Group prayer and feedback	30 minutes
Break	15 minutes
D. Group learnings	20 minutes

Model 2: Peer Group Supervision during Retreats

A second model of peer group supervision can be used during directed or guided retreats, or when a group of spiritual directors who meet regularly are learning together to give the retreat in everyday life to individuals. This model differs from the first model in several ways: (1) it allows time for more than one director to present; (2) usually verbal, not written, presentations are made; and (3) a presenting director moves immediately to inner experience with little reference made to the retreatant. The following is a description of the format and components of this model.

Format and Components

A. Determination of presenters

Participants state who needs to present during this peer group time. For instance, in a group of five, three directors may need to present on a given day.

B. Presentation by first director

The first presenter shares succinctly the inner experience or issue he or she needs to process.

The group helps the presenter to unpack his or her experience in a contemplative and evocative way.

C. Group prayer and feedback

After a moment of quiet prayer, each participant may share an observation, insight, or suggestion with the presenter.
Each sharing must be brief.

Presentation by Second Director, Group Prayer, and Feedback

(Same principles and procedure as above)

Presentation by Third Director, Group Prayer, and Feedback

(Same principles and procedure as above)

The peer group session continues in this manner until every director who has expressed a need to present has an opportunity to share within the given time frame of the peer group session.

If there is sufficient time one or more directors may express a feeling about their own experience that emerged as the session unfolded. The group may also want to share significant insights gained or reaffirmed about God, religious or life experience, or the dynamics involved in offering retreats.

Dynamics and Atmosphere

1. Constant prayer

Directors pray before, during, and after the peer group session, asking God to be present at each moment. They strive to be attentive to the guiding presence of the Spirit at all times during the supervision session.

2. A contemplative atmosphere

    A reverent and spacious atmosphere permeates the session. The directors have a spirit of reverence for the interior experience of the presenting director, providing the space for the director to ponder and get in touch with feelings. The session, at its best, is unrushed and characterized by a free-flowing quality.

3. An evocative stance

    Supervisors help the presenter's feelings and insights to surface at their own pace. Their stance needs to be an inviting one to facilitate a gradual unfolding of the director's inner experience and to allow a reverential revelation of unresolved issues.

4. A focused approach

    A clear focus on the director's inner experience during the exploratory part of the session is essential. The supervising directors assist the presenting director in remaining focused on his or her interior experience and in moving to deeper feelings and insights.

    The group stays focused on one area, issue, or range of feelings at a time until each topic has reached its completion or revealed itself fully. "For it is not much knowledge that fills and satisfies the soul, but the *intimate understanding* and *relish of the truth*" (*Spiritual Exercises,* 2).

5. Quiet moments; prayerful pauses

    Pauses and quiet moments permeate the entire session in order to allow for deeper and nonthreatening inner exploration to occur.

Role of the Facilitator

The facilitator performs several tasks, including keeping time; reminding the group of the approach to take; fostering an unrushed, contemplative atmosphere; maintaining focus on the director's expressed need and inner experience; and encouraging contemplative pauses when necessary. The facilitator invites the group to enter into moments of quiet reflection to help the director become concretely aware of God, to experience feelings more deeply, and to come to greater clarity around an area of struggle or unfreedom.

When the peer group is not part of a training program, frequently the facilitator will be different for each session so that everyone in the group gains experience.

Reminders

At the beginning of a peer group supervision session, it is beneficial for the facilitator to underscore certain principles regarding group supervision. The facilitators could share or simply read the following reminders, beginning each with "Let us remember to . . . . "

1. Be attentive to the guiding presence of the Spirit at all times during the supervision session.

2. Stay focused on the spiritual director's inner experience, not the directee's experience. We look at the directee's experience only to help the director be more in touch with his or her own experience. The director's growing self-awareness and freedom will overflow into future direction sessions.

3. Stay focused on one feeling or issue at a time until its full revelation and completion.

4. Keep the focus on the director in an evocative way during the exploratory portion of the session. We do not offer any insights, comments, or feedback. We will have time for feedback in the third part of the supervision process.

5. Be as contemplative and unrushed as possible, giving the person the time and inner space to experience and address underlying issues. In other words, we allow enough time for the director's interior experience to reveal itself and for God's presence to be felt.

6. Be careful not to ask a question too quickly when a supervisor is helping a director to explore a given reaction or underlying issue.

7. Remain connected while supervising in order to build upon one another's supervision.

Advantages and Disadvantages of Peer Group Supervision

Advantages

1. Various gifts and complementarity of gifts

   The gifts of various supervisors unfold. When one supervisor is feeling stuck or unsure of where to go next, another supervisor can help the presenting director to remain focused on his or her experience.

2. Group prayer and discernment

   The minds and hearts of the supervisors move together in a prayerful and discerning way. A constant attentiveness to God is a pervasive dimension of the session.

3. Growth in patience and self-acceptance

   When spiritual directors come to see they are not alone in their struggles, they grow more patient with themselves and more accepting of their own weaknesses and inadequacies.

4. Valuable feedback offered by the group

During the group feedback portion of the session, the members of the group offer valuable insights, reflections, suggestions, and further questions for the presenting director to ponder. This feedback can be valuable for all of the spiritual directors present as well as for the presenting director.

5. A learning experience for all present

The spiritual directors who are supervising are getting in touch with their own experience. Similar experiences or struggles may arise within their own minds and hearts. They can learn a great deal from the presenting director's experience of direction and supervision.

Also, the group learnings time could be used for further insights into spiritual growth, prayer, spiritual direction, and supervision.

6. A community of spiritual directors

Spiritual directors experience the support of a community of colleagues. They come to feel a oneness with others in the joys and struggles of directing. Fellowship before or after peer group sessions can also deepen the sense of community.

Disadvantages

1. Bond of trust and vulnerability

Individuals may experience difficulty trusting and being vulnerable in a group setting.

2. Possible disconnectedness and disjointedness in the group

   If the group does not move together in a prayerful and discerning way, then the supervision session could move from one reaction or issue to another without adequately exploring any one area, feeling, or issue.

3. Possible competition

   While one member of a group evokes the director's experience at a given moment, the others need to wait patiently for their opportunity to assist the director. The members of the group may work against one another by simultaneously trying to assist the presenting director.

   Further, members may feel that their area of focus is the "best" one, competing with others to have the presenting director remain with a particular area of focus, a specific reaction, or a new insight.

4. Possible lack of depth

   If there is disconnectedness and competition within the group, supervision could lose its depth. Individual supervision can allow for deeper insights, since only one supervisor helps the spiritual director explore.

Being aware of the dynamics and atmosphere of peer group supervision can alleviate any disadvantages that may arise.

Conclusion

Like individual supervision, peer group supervision can be a rich experience of insight and freedom for the presenting spiritual director. It can also be a key learning experience for all of the participants because of the theological reflection component. Participants can learn from one another's struggles and joys of directing. The key is to keep the focus on the presenting director's interior experience and to be very mindful of God's permeating presence during the supervision session. Through a contemplative atmosphere, the living water of God's presence can seep into the minds and hearts of all participants. Therefore, the peer group supervision session can become an experience of God as well as a significant learning experience.

Questions for Reflection and Discussion

For Supervisors

1. How do the two models of peer group supervision presented in this chapter relate to your experience of peer group supervision? Does your approach allow for a significant amount of time to explore the presenting director's inner experience?

2. One of the greatest challenges of peer group supervision is to keep the focus on the director, not on the directee. In your peer group do you find yourselves sometimes moving away from the director's experience to the directee's experience? How can you help the group maintain the proper focus? Be specific and concrete.

3. What advantages and disadvantages of individual and peer group supervision have you discovered?

4. What size group is most helpful for peer group supervision? Why?

5. How do you see the role of the facilitator? Do the members of your peer group rotate being facilitator?

For Spiritual Directors

1. From your experience, what advantages and disadvantages does peer group supervision have over individual supervision? Which do you prefer? Why?

2. Does your peer group work together as a team? What would help your peer group unfold in a teamlike fashion that is supportive of spiritual directors?

3. Is your peer group contemplative and evocative in its approach? What could be done to help your peer group to become more contemplative?

4. How would you describe the role of the facilitator in your group? Do you rotate this role?

5. What insights have you gained from this chapter that could enhance your experience of peer group supervision?

A Contemplative Moment

Remember a time when you experienced a deep sense of communion in your peer group. What was that experience like? What was God like? What qualities were alive in the participants?

Let the memory and grace of that experience flow over you and within you. Thank God for this graced experience.

Ask the Spirit of God to continue to permeate the hearts, minds, and spirits of all members of your group.

Prayer for Unity

God of Communion, thank you for bringing us together in your name to be Eucharist to one another.

When one of us is in pain, help us be a compassionate presence.

When one is in darkness, may we be a vehicle of your light.

When one is in turmoil, may we be an instrument of your peace.

When one is confused, help us be bearers of your wisdom and truth.

Thank you, Companion God, for inviting us to be a support to one another in this sacred ministry. Help us to hold reverently what each person shares. Give us the gift of tender hands and warm hearts to hold one another's vulnerability and weakness.

As we grow in trust of you, help us to grow in trust of one another, believing that all of our work is in your Holy Name.

7

Overwhelmed by
a Directee's Depression:
A Peer Group Supervision
Case Study

Spiritual directors bring directing situations to supervision for a variety of reasons. Spiritual directors, for example, want to discover the experiential reasons for the strong affective reactions they experience during direction sessions. The following peer group supervision session focuses on a spiritual director's intense, anxious, and fearful reactions to the persistent depression of one of her directees. It illustrates the first model of peer group supervision, that for ongoing spiritual direction, which was described in chapter 6.

Four spiritual directors participate in this two-hour supervision session. Mary, the director, presents a verbatim case study on Angie, the directee. Ryan, Pam, and Joan are the three supervisors.

A. Presentation of Case: Director Presents the Background of the Directee and Verbatim

Angie is a thirty-five-year-old married woman with two children who has been receiving spiritual direction every three or four weeks for more than two years. Despite being a very attractive and talented woman, Angie suffers from low self-esteem and lacks self-confidence. Over a thirteen-year period she has been in therapy several times to treat her on-and-off bouts of depression. She has resumed therapy during the past six months.

Angie's depression episodes vary in intensity. Sometimes she feels hopeful. Other times she is close to despair. Although she has not actually attempted suicide, Angie occasionally has strong suicidal feelings. Through therapy and spiritual direction, however, her "light" periods last longer than her "dark" periods.

Angie has a deep desire to grow closer to God and to involve God in her darkness. Over time Angie has been learning to share her feelings openly with God and Mary, her spiritual director. Through spiritual direction and prayer, she has become aware of her emotional perceptions of God: God is an overbearing male; God is aloof and uncaring except to watch what she does wrong; God does not understand or feel her pain. Slowly, through encountering God in a personal way, Angie's experience and image of God have changed. She is beginning to experience God as a caring and loving God, as a God who wants to support her and stay close during her struggles.

Verbatim

The following verbatim describes a *spiritual relapse:* Angie falls back into her distorted image of God. But also it describes a major breakthrough. By honestly sharing her anger with God, Angie again experiences God as caring and loving.

Director's reactions	Conversation
Anxiety	Angie 1: I feel like I am surrounded by a wall that is four feet thick. It's like one of those Indian teepees—it completely surrounds me, and it's four feet thick.
	Mary 1: What is it like for you there?
Slight fear	A2: It's totally dark. I am in complete darkness and all alone. God is nowhere to be found.

	M2:	You're all alone, and God is nowhere to be found.
Glad she notices God somewhere!	A3:	That's right. (She pauses and closes her eyes for a moment.) God is far off in the distance, up there in the sky (points up to her right).
	M3:	God is up there in the sky.
Anxiety/sadness	A4:	Yes, like a statue—aloof, cold, no feeling.
	M4:	Aloof, cold, and no feeling. Can you say more?
Fearful about her disillusionment	A5:	Yes, God is looking down at the world, in a general way; he's not concerned about individuals. It's like he created the world and just lets it unfold without being involved anymore.
	M5:	God is unconcerned and uninvolved.
Fear	A6:	Yes, he's cold and like a statue.
	M6:	How do you feel about God standing there far off—statue-like, without feeling, uninvolved?
	A7:	There's nothing I can do about it. If that's the way God wants to be, then just let him be that way.
	M7:	How do you feel as you say that, "just let him be that way"?
Glad she's feeling anger	A8:	I guess it annoys me. It bothers me, but there is nothing I can do about it. He doesn't care how I feel anyway. (Mary continues to help Angie talk about her powerless and feelings of hopelessness.)
Mixture of hope and fear	M8:	Do you think you could take some time now to tell God—

as God stands there far off, unfeeling, uncaring—how you feel about him? Maybe share with him your angry and hopeless feelings, as you just shared with me? Just take your time. (Angie often has a hard time acknowledging anger and despair. When she does, Mary sometimes invites her to share these feelings with God while they are still alive within her.)

Moved by her tears

(Angie took about eight to ten minutes to express her feelings to God, silently. She cried. Then she shared with Mary what happened.)

A9:   I'm surprised about what just happened. I broke the statue. I couldn't stand God standing there like that—so cold and unfeeling.

M9:   You broke the statue. How did that feel?

Thrilled!

A10:   It felt freeing, like a release of pent-up feelings within me. I told God I couldn't stand him being so distant and aloof. Then something else surprising happened. Another statue came to my mind—a statue of Jesus I made in ceramics class several years ago. I really love it. As I remembered that

Thank you, Lord!

statue, it was like Jesus was standing there with his arms extended toward me. He is smiling. There is a light coming from him. He is aware of me, individually. He seems alive and joyful.

	M10:	Gosh, what a grace! (Pause) So Jesus is aware of you individually, and he is smiling.
Moved by Jesus' concern	A11:	Yes, it's like he's happy to be with me and really cares about what happens to me.
	M11:	How does that feel—that Jesus is happy to be with you and cares about what happens to you?
Grateful	A12:	(Tearful) I feel moved by that, moved that he really cares. I don't feel as alone. I feel cared for and more connected with him.

(Mary and Angie contemplate this experience for a while. Angie leaves the session that day feeling as if a burden has been lifted.)

Reason for Presenting This Situation

Although feeling great joy and delight over Angie's experience of Jesus' loving presence, Mary wants to explore the effect of Angie's depression on herself. Because Angie's depression is so intense at times, Mary sometimes becomes fearful that both she and Angie will be overwhelmed by the strength of the depression.

Mary is usually confident in God's presence and assistance during a direction session and trusts that the depression will not overwhelm Angie and herself. However, during the early stages of this session, Angie's depression was so strong that Mary found herself caught in the darkness and losing confidence in God's supportive presence. She wanted to unpack her own fear.

B. Group Exploration:
Contemplative and Evocative

Through an evocative and contemplative approach, the three supervisors help Mary savor the breakthrough Angie experienced in the direction session and to explore her own fears about being overwhelmed by the darkness of Angie's depression. Mary shares the following account of the supervision session.

Mary's Account

Mary: With Joan, Pam, and Ryan, I shared my two reactions during the direction session. One strong reaction was my *fear and trepidation* because of Angie's darkness. Total darkness seemed to pervade Angie as she talked about the four-foot wall and her unconcerned and distant God.

My other feeling was *confidence*—I felt God surrounding both of us, although Angie had a four-foot wall of darkness surrounding her.

As I described my inner experience, Joan, Pam, and Ryan felt that *my fear was stronger than my confidence*. Their prayerful discernment moved them to help me to explore my fear and trepidation. With the help of my supervisors I was able to explore Angie's darkness and its effect on me. Her darkness felt so despairing, totally hopeless, barren, and powerful, and she seemed so caught in this darkness. I was very fearful that I would get caught in its despairing power, too.

(During the session, as they continued to explore the darkness, an image appeared to Mary.)

Mary 1: (Slowly) An image is coming to my mind of a whirlpool swirling around in a rough ocean. Angie is right in the middle of that whirlpool and going deeper into the darkness. She's caught, and I'm on the outskirts of the darkness. I'm fearful of getting caught in it.

Pam 1: You're fearful of getting caught in the whirlpool.

M2: Yes, Angie is caught in this whirlpool, being pulled down deeper and getting more caught in the throes of darkness. And I'm going down with her. That's scary.

P2: Yeah, it really sounds scary—you feel like you're caught in the whirlpool with Angie and being pulled down with her.

M3: Yes, but I notice that I'm more in the current rather than in the eye of the whirlpool. I'm more on the outskirts of the whirlpool.

P3: You're on the outskirts of the whirlpool. How do you feel there?

M4: I feel relieved. I'm not caught in the depth of the depression and darkness that Angie is experiencing. I feel such relief that I am not in the eye of the whirlpool, that Angie's darkness is not totally overwhelming me.

P4: You feel very relieved. I can sense your relief as you're saying it.

M5: Yes, I don't feel as afraid at the moment. (Pauses) But, even though I am more in the current than in the eye of the whirlpool, black tar water is splashing forcefully over me, like muddy waters.

Ryan 1: How does that feel, Mary, having black tar water splash over you?

M6: Well, it's a little scary, but not as scary as feeling caught in the eye of the whirlpool.

R2: A little scary.

M7: Yes. (Pauses) However, as that black tar water splashes over me, and it's real forceful, I'm noticing a light within me. It probably sounds funny, but it's as if I'm a light-bulb that's lit. The black tar water splashes over me, but the light within me stays on.

R3: The light within you stays on.

M8: Yes. The light is a feeling of confidence and hope, that even though the darkness is overwhelming at times, I have a deep sense that Angie is going to be all right. I wasn't feeling that before.

Joan 1: Do you know what's causing that deep sense within you?

M9: (Slowly) You know, as you ask, I see the hand of God at the bottom of the whirlpool, ready to catch Angie and me. God is right there, in the depths of the ocean, with his hand open, ready to catch us. God's hand is very ten-der, yet very strong. It is there waiting to catch Angie in her darkness. (She contemplates God's hand for a while.)

Gosh, this is truly powerful! I feel different seeing God's hand there.

J2:   You feel different.

M10:Yes, I feel like a burden is lifted. Neither Angie nor I are going to drown or be overcome by the darkness of this black whirlpool. God's tender and strong hand is there to catch us. Gosh, that makes me feel lighter!

J3:   You really feel lighter seeing God's hand there.

M11: Yes, I can really *feel* that God's power is going to prevail. Where before I only talked about it, today I *knew* and *believed* it. I feel so much freer of my fears about whether myself or Angie is going to be overwhelmed by her depression.

J4:   That's great that you feel much freer, Mary.

M12:Yes, I feel lighthearted now. Free. Joy. Even if Angie sinks down into the depths of the whirlpool, God's strong and loving hand is there to catch her. This is a very powerful moment for me. I feel much more confidence and hope now. I feel this confidence and light-heartedness will be with me when I see Angie for direction next week.

I'm feeling deeply grateful that God revealed himself to me so vividly and powerfully during this supervision session. Thank you for helping me to talk out my feelings and to notice God's presence through that image.

C. Group Prayer and Feedback:
A Major Point, Feeling, or Question for Further Consideration, after a Period of Quiet Reflection

Ryan: I am most struck, and really overwhelmed, by the way God so vividly broke through your darkness—God's hand was right there to catch both of you as the whirlpool pulled you down. I could feel a difference in you when you noticed God's hand there—your heaviness and worry changed to a lightness and confidence. Your eyes and posture changed. I feel delighted for you that God broke through in this way.

I suggest that you be very conscious of God's hand holding both of you, particularly when Angie walks into your office depressed and weighed down.

Joan: I too am touched by God's hand being there for you. The darkness felt so strong and heavy as you described it, yet I sensed God was in it somewhere. I'm glad we explored that darkness so that you could notice God's presence. You seem so lighthearted now.

Pam: I just want to say thank you, Mary. This helped me so much, gave me confidence, to see how God can change such heavy feelings. I could feel your heaviness when you explored the darkness and shared your fear that Angie's depression would overwhelm both of you. I felt heavy. But I noticed a change in you when you saw God's hand. And I felt lighter, too. Thank you. Your sharing today gives me greater confidence with a few of my directees that are experiencing strong resistance and heavy problems.

Mary: I feel like a different person. I cannot begin to tell you the confidence and hope I feel seeing God's strong and loving hand so vividly. I feel such strong confidence now that the depth of Angie's darkness cannot overcome God's light.

I will bring this powerful experience with me when I am in a direction session with Angie. By remembering God's strong hand waiting to catch Angie, I feel that I can be freer to be with her in an unblocked way. When my fears begin to arise again when Angie's depression is strong, I have confidence now that God's tender hand, ready to catch Angie, will help to relieve my fears and restore my confidence that God's light will prevail over darkness.

D. Group Learnings:
Key Insights about Prayer, Spiritual Direction, Supervision, and the *Spiritual Exercises*

The group shares the following insights gained and reaffirmed during this supervision session.

1. Prayer and spiritual direction

    a) By helping directees to examine more closely a nega-
        tive image of God (see Mary 2–Angie 7), directors
        can help them *feel their feelings* toward that image
        and express these feelings to God. This expression
        can open them to God's true revelation of Self.

    b) In addition to directors encouraging directees to
        express their feelings to God on their own, directors
        can also invite them to share their feelings with God
        during a direction session when (1) a directee has
        had a difficult time getting in touch with his or her
        negative feelings; and (2) a director senses that a
        directee's expression of strong feelings can allow him
        or her to notice God's felt presence.

2. Supervision

    a) By exploring and unpacking an area of darkness
        with others, a spiritual director can feel God's pres-
        ence, which gives the director confidence in future
        direction sessions where resistance might be strong.

    b) Supervisors need to be discerning in order to dis-
        cover the strongest movement and/or countermove-
        ment for the director to unpack.

    c) Just as spiritual direction allows directees to explore
        resistance and to notice God's presence, so does
        supervision free spiritual directors from negative feel-
        ings. This freedom enables them to be more fully
        present to their directees, a presence in which they
        listen with free hearts, not cluttered hearts.

3. Insights from the *Spiritual Exercises*

    a) Repetition (Rules 62 and 118): "Attention should
        always be given to some more important parts which

one has experienced understanding, consolation, or desolation" (118). This dynamic of lingering with and exploring areas of consolation and desolation applies in all three areas: the directee's prayer, the direction session, and supervision.

b) Even though desolation can conceal God's felt presence, God is still very present.

Through unpacking the desolation, a directee or a director can again become aware of God's affective presence.

c) Rule 326, referring to bringing hidden realities out into the light in the presence of a "spiritual" person, is experienced in both the spiritual direction and supervision sessions.

Conclusion

Mary, the spiritual director, gives Angie, the directee, the opportunity to share her anger with God and to talk about it. This expression of "repressed affectivity" helps free Angie to see God as a loving God. She feels lighter, less burdened as she leaves spiritual direction that day. Truly a graced moment for Angie!

In peer group supervision Mary talks out her fear of being overwhelmed by Angie's depression. Her supervisors contemplatively and evocatively help Mary look into the well of her interior experience to understand her anxiety and fear, to explore the reasons underneath those feelings, and to recognize God's presence. These experiential insights help Mary restore her confidence and regain her inner freedom when she is with Angie. Truly a graced experience for Mary!

Questions for Reflection and Discussion

For Supervisors

1. How would you describe the atmosphere and approach of the group during peer group supervision?

2. What touches you about the exploratory part of the peer group session? (If you are discussing these questions with a group, read this section aloud.) How would you help Mary savor or explore if you were in the group?

3. What strikes you about the feedback section? the learnings section?

4. When you facilitate a peer group, in what specific ways do you foster a contemplative atmosphere? How does your group respond to your attempts to keep the session in a contemplative mode?

5. Can you remember a peer group supervision session during which the sense of God became very alive in a concrete way? What was that experience like? What was God's presence like? How did this sense of God help the person presenting?

For Spiritual Directors

1. What strikes you about Angie's depression? Have you ever worked with a directee who was depressed? What were some of your feelings and concerns? What did you learn from the experience?

2. What touches you about Angie's experience of a lively God? (If discussing these questions with a group, two people should read the spiritual direction conversation aloud.) What do you notice about Mary's approach and her responses during the spiritual direction session? What

part of Angie's experience would you stay with if you were her director?

3. Do you remember a supervision session in which you were the presenting director when a major shift occurred? What were you presenting? How would you describe the shift? What was God's presence like during the session? How would you describe the atmosphere in the group? What insights did you gain from this experience?

4. How have prayerful pauses helped you during peer group supervision? What happens to the session and the group when these pauses are not present?

5. What do you find to be the most rewarding aspects of peer group supervision? the most challenging?

A Contemplative Moment

Find a rock, either one you can hold or one large enough to sit upon. Touch it, feel it. Notice its impenetrable quality, its solidness, its immovability when firmly placed. Feel its strength and timelessness.

Think of a prolonged struggle in your own life or in the life of someone in your care. Ask God to give you or that person those qualities of solidness, constancy, strength, and eternity that the rock possesses as you journey with this seemingly eternal struggle.

Ask Jesus for the grace not to give up on yourself or the other person, just as he did not give up on the woman at the well, nor on you.

Prayer for a Faithful Heart

God of faithfulness, thank you for always being with us and not giving up on us. Thank you for being our strength in times of weakness, our stronghold in times of powerlessness, our light in times of darkness, our hope in times of despair.

Dear God, I ask for a faithful heart like yours that does not give up on myself or another when all seems lost. I ask for a constancy of love that remains immovable even when raging waters buffet it.

Give me the grace to be faithful to those in my care who experience prolonged pain, knowing that you will sustain me—you who are my rock, my fortress, my stronghold in time of need.

8

Developing a Discerning Heart: Seven Phases of the Supervision Experience

The more attentive and reflective spiritual directors are during spiritual direction and supervision, the deeper will be their level of self-understanding. The more specific their self-awareness and self-knowledge, the more complete will be their growth in interior freedom. In other words, with keener discerning hearts and minds, they will be able to assist their directees' growth in their relationship with God.

This chapter describes the spiritual director's development of a discerning heart by outlining the seven phases of the supervision experience. With each phase, reflection questions are proposed to assist spiritual directors' attentiveness, self-awareness, understanding, discernment, and self-supervision. Chapter 8 also reviews the major points of previous chapters.

First Phase: Prayerful Preparation before a Direction Session

Sometimes the way spiritual directors feel before a direction session may help them to notice movement or countermovement in themselves or in their directee. Questions they can ask themselves to facilitate this awareness include the following.

- How am I feeling about this person coming today? anxious? agitated? glad? excited? peaceful? neutral?

- Do I notice any movement away, such as anxiety, fear, agitation, dread, feelings of inadequacy? Is this movement away because of something this person has been facing? some resistance in him or her? some resistance in me?

- Am I able to articulate in my own mind what I am feeling and my reasons for those feelings?

- Have I asked God to be with us today during direction?

- Have I asked God for a particular grace that I may need to companion this person?

Second Phase: Attentiveness during the Direction Session

During direction sessions, spiritual directors need to be aware of three interrelated areas—their directees' experiences, their own interior movements, and God's presence. In relation to the supervision experience, they need to stay attuned to their own spontaneous emotions. Sometimes they know their reactions and feelings; at other times they can feel but are unable to identify particular reactions and the underlying issues until after the session is completed. Whether during or after the session, they need to be aware that interior reactions (or lack of reactions) are occurring so that they do not unknowingly move directees away from their experience of life and of God.

Although spiritual directors may not be fully aware of their inner life during a direction session, they need to have some semblance of awareness (preconscious or subliminally conscious) of interior movements occurring within them. Otherwise they may become self-absorbed, when they should be self-aware. Self-awareness allows them to acknowledge their reactions and stay with directees' experiences rather than causing distraction by getting caught in their own reactions.

Directors can develop a growing awareness of their own reactions during direction session by

- praying for the grace of self-awareness and the gift of a discerning heart;

- developing attentiveness to include their own interior life as well as their directee's experience and God's affective presence; and

- visualizing each direction session to include the directee, self, and God and envisioning that image in prayer before the session begins.

Third Phase: Prayerful Reflection after a Direction Session

After direction sessions, spiritual directors must reflect prayerfully and contemplatively on the direction experience—that is, envision God and themselves looking together at their time with a directee (see learning experiences 2 and 4 for ways to pray with direction experiences). This contemplative pondering enables them to

- identify specific feelings and feel more deeply;

- notice and savor God's presence;

- gain understanding or felt insights *(sentir)* of the experiential reasons and issues underneath their affective reactions; and

- gain greater clarity into areas of unfreedom that prevent them from empathizing with directees' experiences.

During this prayerful reflection they may write down in their spiritual direction log significant aspects of the direction session, including the dialogue that takes place between the directee and themselves and their own reactions at given moments. In God's presence, spiritual directors can contemplate a direction session with the following questions in mind:

- In general, how was I feeling during this direction session? bored? restless? joyful? peaceful?

- How was I feeling at given moments? at the beginning? in the middle? at the end? when the directee was resistant?

- Were there any strong affective responses occurring in me then or now?

- Was I feeling involved in the person's experience? moved? consoled? joyful? grateful? serene? connected?

- Were there any moments when I felt emotionally distant? distracted? detached? restless? bored? agitated? frustrated? anxious? disconnected?

- Do I know what lies underneath these dissonant feelings? For instance, are there any deeper feelings, prejudices, or attitudes present? an unresolved issue in my life perhaps? an area of vulnerability?

- Did I feel God's presence? What was that presence like? When was God's presence the strongest? the most alive? the most vivid?

- Did I experience a lack of God's presence at any particular moment? Did I lose sight of God? Do I know why?

- Was I listening in a contemplative and evocative way?

- Was I working too hard? Did I move into problem-solving or advice-giving modes? Do I know what was going on inside of me that moved me to any of these stances?

Fourth Phase: Writing a Verbatim on a Session

Spiritual directors may have a number of direction sessions that they can bring to supervision. They need to discern which direction session will be most helpful to explore in supervision and which ones they can leave for self-supervision. This discernment is based on areas of struggle, resistance, and strong feelings within the directors themselves. Therefore questions for directors to ponder include the following:

- In which direction session did I experience very strong affective reactions?

- In which session did I experience within myself stronger than usual resistance or countermovement? During which session did I experience confusion about which direction to follow? about how to help a directee? During which session did I struggle to remain with a directee's experience of life and/or God?

- Was there any direction session that precipitated my own vulnerable issues? How did this affect the session? Do I need to process what happened in me?

- During which session did God seem most absent? most present?

- During which session did I work especially hard?

Spiritual directors' verbal responses are indicators of what is happening interiorly at given moments. Often as directors write a verbatim on a specific part of the conversation, they begin to notice more about their verbal responses and interior reactions. They may experience one or all of the following emotions:

- Become more deeply in touch with their feelings at given moments.

- Gain greater clarity about the sources or reasons for their spontaneous reactions.

- Notice points in the conversation during their own verbal responses where they move the directee away from his or her experience and become aware of what happened within themselves at those moments.

Here are specific questions directors may wish to ask themselves as they write their verbatim.

- When Joan said _____ , how did I feel?

- When I responded with _____ , how did I feel?

- Do I know what in my experience precipitated my verbal response?

- Do I know why I made a particular response, that is, an *experiential why* (letting the reason arise from the experience to my heart, then to my understanding), not an *analytical why* (understanding it from an intellectual perspective only)?

Fifth Phase: Individual or Peer Group Supervision

To help spiritual directors acknowledge their inner life while they are directing, supervisors could ask any of the questions mentioned in the fourth phase. They can also help directors explore their feelings and reasons underlying those feelings by asking them about their verbal responses:

- How did you feel when you asked Mary _____ ?

- How did you feel when you were giving Ryan advice on the verbatim rather than listening to his story?

- How do you feel now about your rather pedantic response?

Supervisors can ask directors about their felt reactions as a directee shares his or her experiences. A supervisor may ask, for example, the following question:

- "What went on inside of you when Glenn said, 'I feel like I do not belong to God or anyone else'?"

Other issues to consider:

- Can you elaborate on the fear you felt when Mary mentioned that Jesus embraced the leper?

- You felt frustrated when Ryan said, "Nothing happened in my prayer this week." Why?

- Can you say more about your frustration? Can you say more about your excited feeling when Amy said she felt like God was surrounding her?

- Let's stay with your agitated feeling when you said _____.

Supervisors can help directors to notice God's felt presence or seeming absence during a direction session by asking questions such as these:

- Did you think of calling on God when Jim seemed to be stuck?

- Were you aware of God's presence when Jane shared that powerful experience? What was God's presence like there?

- At what moment in the session did you feel God's presence the strongest? What was that presence like? How did you feel?

As spiritual directors become more vividly aware of God in a direction session, they often grow more affectively in tune with their deeper self and the experience of the directee. Supervisors can assist this deeper awareness by inviting directors to delve further into their experience:

- Having experienced God as a supportive companion during this direction session, how does that affect your feelings of inadequacy?

- Having realized that God sees you as an important person in your directee's growth, as a channel for God's Spirit, how does that affect your feelings of not being needed in this situation?

- Having noticed more clearly God's deep love for and patience with your directee, how do you feel now toward this person? what has happened to your frustration?

Supervisors assist directors in making concrete applications to a direction session by returning to the verbatim after exploring their reactions.

- Having processed everything, how might you respond now to the director's comment in C14?

- How do you feel about that response?

- Would you say anything differently now? Let's role-play it.

The fifth phase usually takes place during an individual or peer group supervision session. However, for various reasons spiritual directors may need to do this phase on their own through self-supervision. If so, they can consider the areas discussed above by asking themselves the same questions.

Sixth Phase: Prayerful Reflection on a Supervision Session

Through prayerful and written reflection on a supervision session, spiritual directors gain even clearer insight and deeper understanding (see learning experience 7 for three examples). By contemplating what was explored during the supervision session and by reflecting on their supervisor's written comments on the verbatim and verbal feedback, they gain clarity around specific affective reactions and personal issues that influenced the session.

Here are questions they can ask themselves during this prayerful reflection.

- What are the significant issues that surfaced during supervision? areas of struggle or resistance? personal issues affecting my relationship with this directee or the way I am companioning him or her?

- What insights arose about me as a person or as a director? How clear are they to me? What needs greater clarity?

- What became clearer about my moving away from the directee's experience? What are the underlying reasons for that movement?

- What issues or areas of unfreedom do I need to bring to prayer and to my own spiritual direction?

- Specifically, where or how did I grow in greater interior freedom through this supervision session?

- What did I notice about God's presence in the direction session I presented?

- What specific awarenesses or insights surfaced about God and God's presence?

- What grace(s) do I need to ask God for in order to help this person and others grow closer to God?

- What realizations are clearer about my directee's experience of God? life? prayer? resistance?

- What experiential insights became clearer and deeper about religious experience, spiritual growth, significant life issues, the spiritual direction process, supervision?

Seventh Phase: Application of Insights

Finally, spiritual directors come full circle as they prepare for and engage in future direction sessions. Often they feel a greater freedom going into the next session with the directee they presented in supervision. They enter into the session with insights that will enable them to stay with the directee, even when he or she resists God and avoids deeper spiritual growth. Directors come away with specific realizations and tools that will enable them to delve deeper with the directee and will help them create a more contemplative atmosphere. In doing so, they may reflect on specific questions:

- Having seen (identify insights and areas of unfreedom within oneself), how do I hope to be with this directee in future direction sessions?

- How do I hope to approach and stay with difficult issues when the directee brings them up again?

- In what specific ways can I help myself avoid a problem-solving stance again?

- How can I keep a clear inner space when I sense this directee is projecting certain realities onto me?

- In what specific ways can I keep a contemplative stance when I sense a person's strong affection for me?

- What can help me to stay in tune with God when the directee resists again? Can I return to any specific image or sense of God's presence that I savored during supervision?

Supervision has a rippling effect: what directors learn about themselves as persons and as spiritual directors through one direction and supervision session overflows into sessions with

other directees. For instance, the insights and freedom a director gains in processing the fear of a directee's intense anger at
God will flow over into direction sessions with other directees
who are angry at God. Similarly, the insights and freedom
acquired during supervision about working with a directee
who was sexually abused will extend to other directees who
have also been sexually abused. In sum, while considering
their total experience of directing, spiritual directors may
reflect on pertinent questions, such as the following:

- Having seen how easily I can fall into a teaching mode,
  what insights did I gain that can help me counteract this
  tendency in other direction sessions?

- Having realized this area of vulnerability within me
  (identify it), how do I hope to be different in presence
  and approach when a directee is dealing with a similar
  struggle?

- Having realized my lack of knowledge and feelings of
  inadequacy as a directee deals with a particular issue (for
  example, sexual abuse, midlife transition, or codependency), what can I do to help myself become more
  knowledgeable and competent when directees are struggling and praying with troublesome issues?

Conclusion

Through these seven phases of supervision, spiritual directors
develop a keener discerning heart. They delve more deeply
into the well of their interior life of direction experiences.
Through their own reflection and with the help of supervision, they notice more concretely their pure and polluted
inner areas. This specific self-awareness enables them to be
completely engrossed in their directees' experiences of
God and less self-absorbed. Consequently, God's life can
reach greater fullness in their directees and in themselves:
"I have come that you may have life and have it to the full"
(Jn 10:10).

Questions for Reflection and Discussion

For Supervisors

1. What strikes you about these seven phases of the supervision experience? Do you feel that each of these phases are important? What do you notice when a director leaves one or several of them undone?

2. Do your supervisees engage in all seven phases? Do they prepare a written reflection on each supervision session?

3. What kinds of situations do your supervisees usually bring to supervision? Do you sense that they are carefully discerning which situation or experience to bring to each session (fourth phase)? What can you do to help their discerning process at this juncture?

4. Do you ask your supervisees if they pray over their direction experiences and, if so, how they pray? Do you suggest ways for them to pray with their experiences?

5. Do you encourage your supervisees to use the self-supervision process for challenging direction situations that are not explored during individual and peer group supervision because of time limitations?

For Spiritual Directors

1. Do you engage in each of these seven phases? Which ones do you tend to omit? Which ones do you always engage in? What value is there in completing all phases?

2. Do you take the time to pray with your direction experiences? What differences do you notice in yourself when you do? What are the blessings of praying with challenging direction experiences? Reflect on a particularly difficult directee or situation in which you spent time in prayer. What were the fruits of your prayer?

3. Do you prepare a written reflection on your supervision sessions? What are the specific advantages of doing so?

4. Do you undergo self-supervision on challenging direction sessions that you do not bring to supervision? What important insights about yourself as a spiritual director have become clearer through self-supervision?

5. If you have engaged in the process of self-supervision, what advantages and disadvantages have you discovered?

6. Recall when you took the time to work through all seven phases of the supervision experience. What significant insights did you gain about yourself? your directee? God? What was God's presence, or lack of affective presence, like at various phases of this process? How did entering into this full process assist the work with your directee?

A Contemplative Moment

Recall a spiritual direction session when your heart, your directee's heart, and God's heart were all in tune with one another. How would you describe each of your hearts? How did this experience, and others like it, assist your development of a discerning heart?

With God, hold and contemplate your heart when it is most discerning. What is your heart like? What is the discernment like?

Now hold and contemplate your heart when it is least discerning. What is it like? How do you feel?

Feel the difference between the two stances, and ask God for the gift of a growing and open discerning heart.

Prayer for a Discerning Heart

God of inspiration, I ask you for the gift of a discerning heart,
>a heart that remains attentive to you,
>a heart that moves with your Spirit,
>a heart that is aware of its sinfulness,
>a heart that is open to your inspiration and guidance.

Help me to listen with a loving heart to the rich experiences of those in my care. Help me to enter into their struggles and peaceful experiences, their sorrows and joys, their woundedness and their wholeness, their emptiness and their fullness.

As "heart speaks to heart," may it be your heart that touches both our hearts, so that the grace of a discerning heart can come alive in us.

9

The Supervisor's Discerning Heart: Reflecting on the Supervision Experience

Because supervision, as spiritual direction, is a God-centered and contemplative experience, supervisors must develop a prayerful discerning stance as they grow in the knowledge and experience of the supervision process. Learning to be a supervisor requires a clear focus, appropriate use of supervision skills, and a keen self-awareness. The more fine-tuned supervisors become in the use of their supervision skills and awareness of their own inner experience, the more discerning they will become as supervisors in helping the total development of spiritual directors. To develop a discerning heart, supervisors must reflect on their experience of supervising just as spiritual directors must reflect on their experience of directing. They, too, must look into the well of their interior space of supervision experiences. With Jesus as their companion they must dip into, sift apart, and contemplate particular supervision sessions to develop a more precise and discerning approach. This chapter describes three dimensions of discernment that supervisors need for their development: (1) the growth of the spiritual director; (2) the supervision experience itself; and (3) the supervisor's inner experience and stance while supervising.

Two perspectives are crucial to the supervision process. Perspective I includes questions that the supervisor can reflect on and pray with *after each supervision session.* These questions can be used as an awareness examen (see learning experience 10) to assist prayerful discernment and growth in experiential knowledge. Perspective II reflects on the overall experience of supervising a particular spiritual director and includes questions for *periodic reflection* and *self-evaluation.* Learning experiences 9 and 11 are also reflection tools to further assist the supervisor's development of a prayerful discerning heart.

Perspective I: Reflection after Each Supervision Session

Spiritual Director's Experience

The supervisor must be aware of the spiritual director's inner experience and growth both as a director and as a person. This awareness will enable the supervisor to recognize patterns of interior movements, significant issues that continue to emerge for the director, and overall areas of growth in the director's self-knowledge and freedom. The following questions can facilitate this process.

Interior Movements

1. What were the main countermovements explored during this session? What were the experiential reasons underlying these countermovements?

2. Were any consoling movements savored? If so, did these movements enhance the director's growth?

3. Was there a difference in the affectivity of the spiritual director as the session progressed? Describe the difference(s).

4. In what specific way did the director acknowledge God's presence or absence during the direction session? Did the director contemplate God's affective presence (or notice God's absence) during the supervision session?

What was God's presence or absence like? Specifically, what effect did contemplating God's presence have on the director?

Areas of Unfreedom and Vulnerable Issues

1. How would you identify the situation/experience that the spiritual director brought to the session? What affective responses surfaced in the director?

2. Were there any areas of unfreedom or vulnerable personal issues that emerged? If so, is it an area or issue that has surfaced previously? Has there been any growth in the director's awareness and freedom?

3. Did this unfree area prevent the spiritual director from staying with the directee's experience or exploring it more deeply? If so, was this apparent to the director in the spiritual direction conversation?

Growth in Freedom and Practical Applications

1. Did you see or sense any growth in the director's interior freedom from the beginning to the end of the session? What was the new freedom that emerged?

2. What practical applications did the spiritual director make to future direction sessions with the directee and with others?

Significant Insights

1. What felt knowledge (felt insights) did the spiritual director gain as a director? as a person?

2. What insights about religious experience, spiritual direction, and/or supervision were gained or reaffirmed through this supervision session?

3. Regarding which human issues (for example, addiction, depression, midlife transition) or areas related to spiritual direction does the director need additional knowledge?

Did you suggest ways and resources through which this knowledge can be acquired?

The Supervision Experience

Supervisors also must monitor the supervision experience itself by reflecting on the focus, purposes, process, and skills of supervising a spiritual director. Taking time to do this reflection after each supervision session enables them to learn the nuances of focus and purpose and the practical dimensions of process and skills. Insights gained in one supervision session carry over into supervision sessions with other directors. The following are questions to assist supervisors' reflection on particular supervision sessions.

Supervision Purposes and Focus

1. Did the focus remain with the spiritual director's inner experience? If yes, how did this focus bear fruit?

2. Did you help the director see how his or her inner experience affected responses to the directee?

3. At any point during the session did the focus move away from the director's experience? When and how did that happen? Did the focus eventually return to the director's experience? When did you become aware of this movement away—was it during the session or at this particular moment?

4. What might you do differently to remain focused on the director's experience?

Contemplative Process and Presence

1. How did you foster a contemplative atmosphere during the supervision session? Was the supervision experience one of reverently drawing water from the well of the spiritual director's interior directing space? If yes, in what

specific ways? If no, can you describe what the experience was like?

2. Were the spiritual director and you aware of God's presence during the supervision session? What was the sense of God's felt presence (or absence) like?

3. Did you help the spiritual director savor God's affective presence and explore God's seeming absence in the direction session that was brought to supervision?

Supervision Skills

1. What skills mostly applied during the session: listening? exploring? practical application and role-playing? feedback? How specifically were each of these skills used?

2. Are you satisfied with the various skills that were used? Were there any skills you could have used more or better? During which moments of the session could you have used particular skills more effectively?

Supervisor's Inner Experience and Stance

Supervisors also must be aware of their own inner experience and stance during and after each supervision session. They, as spiritual directors, experience various interior movements during the sessions. Their own vulnerable and unresolved issues may be stirred as spiritual directors process their experience. For example, as a spiritual director processes a fear of failure with a given directee, the supervisor also may notice a strong fear of failure. Or a supervisor may experience feelings of frustration and become aggressive with a director who is slow to recognize an inner experience. Further, a supervisor may be experiencing countertransference reactions with a given director. In order to be free and fully present with supervisees, supervisors need to be aware of their inner experience and process it within themselves and/or with another supervisor. The following questions can assist supervisors' awareness of their interior life and stance during and after a supervision session.

Supervisor's Interior Movements

1. What affective reactions surfaced in you during the session: excitement? joy? a feeling of congruence? satisfaction? frustration? impatience? anxiety? fear? Do you know the experiential reasons underlying each of these reactions? Where in your body do you feel the stronger reactions?

2. What happened with any negative feelings that surfaced in you? Did they interfere with you being fully present to the director? Were you able to "clear a space" within you in order to be fully present? How did you do this?

3. What was the strongest consolation during or after the session? the strongest desolation? Do you know the reason for the desolate movement within you?

Areas of Unfreedom and Vulnerable Issues

1. Did the spiritual director's experience precipitate any of your own areas of darkness or vulnerable issues? What specific areas or issues were being touched within you? What feelings surfaced around each of these issues?

2. Were you aware that an area of unfreedom was triggered within you during the supervision session or now as you reflect? If during the session, what did you do in the moment in order to stay focused on the director?

3. What do you need to do to process any issues that were touched? Do you need additional time in prayer, for example? Do you need to discuss it with someone? Would it help to jot down thoughts in a journal or do some type of physical exercise?

God's Presence

1. Did you remember to pray before the supervision session for both yourself and the spiritual director? Did you notice any effect that your prayerful approach, or lack of it, had on the session?

2. What was God's affective presence, or seeming lack of presence, like for you during this session? Where and how did God seem to be working in and through you for the well-being of the director?

3. Was there any moment during the session that you experienced a need for God's assistance? Did you call on God then? What happened as you called on God?

4. Describe a moment of grace that occurred for you during the supervision session.

Supervisor's Stance

1. How present were you to the spiritual director's experience? Where were you listening from: your mind? your emotions? your imagination? your interior space? several of these? How would you describe your way of listening?

2. How were you present with the spiritual director's resistance? Were you reverent? contemplative? evocative? challenging? confrontative? problem solving? advice giving? pushy? How do you feel about your presence and approach during this session?

Significant Insights

1. What insights about the supervision purposes, focus, process, and skills did you gain or were reaffirmed?

2. Are there any areas related to spiritual direction, supervision, or human issues about which you need further knowledge? How can you grow in this knowledge?

Perspective II: Periodic Reflection on Supervision

In addition to reflecting on each supervision session, supervisors can also benefit from a periodic reflection (possibly two or three times a year) of their supervision experience with each spiritual director. This reflection can improve their awareness of significant areas of growth in themselves as supervisors as well as in their supervisees. The following questions may help.

A Spiritual Director's Growth

1. What situations or experiences does the spiritual director usually bring to supervision? Is there enough variety? Are there some situations or directees that the spiritual director never brings to supervision? Would it be helpful for the person's growth as a spiritual director to address some of these points?

2. What significant and/or unresolved personal issues of the director have been emerging during this period? Besides time spent in supervision, in what ways is the director processing them? How? through prayer? through journaling? through spiritual direction? through counseling? with a close friend?

3. In what specific ways do these issues influence the ability of the director to stay with directees' experiences? Does it affect his or her ability and effectiveness as a spiritual director in any other way?

4. What issues are emerging around the director's contemplative stance and approach to spiritual direction? Is the person able to stay connected with the directees' experiences of God? If not, what is preventing this sense of connection? Is he or she being reverent and compassionate as a listener? evocative in approach? If not, what is preventing either of these from taking place?

5. In what specific ways has the spiritual director developed a discerning heart during this period? At the same

time, in what specific ways does this person need to grow in the art and skill of discernment?

6. What growing edges does the director need to address through supervision in the future? How can you be a caring companion as these growing edges and areas of weakness move into areas of strength?

7. What major insights about religious experience, human issues, spiritual direction, and supervision has the person gained during this period? What knowledge does this person need to improve as a spiritual director?

A Supervisor's Inner Awareness and Growth

1. In general, how well have you been staying focused on the spiritual director's inner experience? What are some specific times and ways that you have maintained this focus? What have been the fruits for the spiritual director? for yourself?

2. How often do you find yourself moving away from the director's experiences to the directee's experiences? When? Why? What would help you to maintain the appropriate focus?

3. When and how do you use the skills of contemplative listening? evocative listening? exploring? practical application? role-playing? feedback? Are there any skills that you rarely use? Can you think of moments during supervision when you could have used those particular skills? What have been the benefits of role-playing for the spiritual director? What role-playing techniques have you found helpful?

4. What is your usual stance with this spiritual director? Do you find yourself talking too much, teaching, offering advice, trying to fix challenging situations? What can you do to adopt a more contemplative and evocative stance during supervision?

5. How aware of God are you during supervision sessions? What has helped you to stay aware of God's presence? How can you help yourself become even more aware?

6. What are some specific insights about the supervision process that you have gained or have had reaffirmed from supervising this spiritual director?

7. How have you been graced or blessed by supervising this person? Can you name several specific blessings?

8. What gifts and skills as a supervisor are you developing and using as a result of supervising this person? What are some growing edges?

9. In what specific ways are you developing a discerning heart? How has supervising this person helped you to grow in the art and skill of discernment?

10. What graces do you need to continue to help this spiritual director through the supervision process?

Conclusion

To develop a discerning heart supervisors must take time to reflect upon and pray with their supervision experiences. They, too, need to sit with Jesus at the well and contemplate the richness of their interior space. Their own experience as supervisors and as spiritual directors can become a fountain providing life for others in their supervisory care. As Jesus says: "The water I give shall become a fountain within you, leaping up to provide God's life" (Jn 4:14). Supervisors' own prayerful reflection and connection with God during supervision can be that fountain, providing God's life for other spiritual directors—life that will seep into directors' hearts and souls so that they can provide a contemplative atmosphere and God-centered focus for their directees.

Questions for Reflection and Discussion

For Supervisors

1. Do you take enough time to prayerfully reflect on your supervision experience with each of the spiritual directors in your care? If not, what can you do to help yourself find adequate time?

2. What benefits do you see (or have seen) in taking the time for prayerful reflection on your supervision experience? Does using the image of yourself and Jesus looking into the well of your supervision experiences help your prayerful reflection?

3. Are there other questions or any other areas of reflection needed besides those mentioned in this chapter?

4. Do you keep notes or a written log on your supervision experiences (see learning experience 8)? If so, what benefits have you seen?

5. Do you periodically evaluate the supervision experience with each of your supervisees? If so, what have you learned about yourself as a supervisor?

For Spiritual Directors

1. How do you feel knowing that your supervisor takes the time for prayerful reflection of your experience in supervision?

2. Have you ever noticed your supervisor becoming frustrated or aggressive with you? Do you know why? Did you discuss it with your supervisor?

3. Do you feel any attraction to offer supervision to spiritual directors? What are some of the feelings and thoughts connected with that attraction?

4. Supervision can be like a fountain offering you God's life to help you in your ministry of spiritual direction. In what specific ways has the supervision process been like the fountain of living waters?

A Contemplative Moment

Recall a supervision session during which your contemplative stance and attentiveness were present. Experience again God's presence and the blessing of this session for both the supervisee and yourself.

Recall a supervision session during which a contemplative atmosphere was lacking. Feel again the lack of God's affective presence and the disjointedness of the session.

Feel and describe the difference between these two sessions.

With God, hold your heart when it was its most attentive and absorbed and ask God to help that contemplative spirit to become a fountain within you and flow over into future supervision sessions.

Prayer for a Contemplative Heart

God of the present moment, thank you for the many moments you give us each day to be aware of life, to enjoy life, to savor the many gifts that are part of life.

Thank you for the many opportunities you give me to help others grow closer to you and to live a more joy-filled life.

I ask you for the grace of a contemplative heart at all moments, but especially in those moments when I am journeying with others. As I sit with people in supervision, help me to be fully present to their unfolding experience and your guiding spirit. Give me an attentive mind, an open heart, and a discerning spirit so that I can be a contemplative companion to spiritual directors as they help directees to contemplate you, and as they delve into their woundedness that prevents them from doing so.

Help me to realize what a privilege it is to be a wounded healer journeying with other wounded healers.

Let the living waters of your gracious presence spring up from within us and wash over our wounds so that we can be even more of a healing presence to others.

10

Supervision As a Learning Experience

In educational programs spiritual directors learn the skills, content, and dynamics of spiritual direction and spiritual growth in a variety of ways that include taking courses, attending workshops, practicing theological reflection, participating in faith-sharing, offering spiritual direction, and receiving supervision. Supervision is the key practical learning experience for spiritual directors. It is an arena for experiential understanding—that is, the "intimate knowledge and relish of the truth" that Ignatius of Loyola mentions in the *Spiritual Exercises*, where theoretical knowledge becomes experiential insights.

This book emphasizes that the focus of supervision lies with the inner experience of spiritual directors as they direct, not on the experience of the directees. The skills of supervision aim toward greater clarity and insight surrounding directors' inner experiences so they can stay with their directees' life and spiritual experience. Therefore, the primary learning experience of supervision is rooted in the spiritual director's own growing self-knowledge. However, the process of supervision can also produce experiential learnings around other areas. There are "teachable moments"; for example, a director may learn a new insight about a particular issue. This chapter describes how supervision is a learning experience for directors as persons and as spiritual directors. Further it explores how supervision is a learning experience for supervisors. It also distinguishes between supervision and consultation.

A Personal Learning Experience for Spiritual Directors

Spiritual directors bring themselves as persons to directing situations. The more they are aware of themselves as individuals, the more authentic they are as spiritual directors. They can relate more genuinely and empathetically with their directees because they too are processing their own issues. Directors are only as developed in their role as spiritual directors as they are caring human beings.

Innate in directors' growing self-knowledge is their developing awareness of specific areas of brokenness, unfreedom, and vulnerable issues. As directees share unresolved issues, areas of struggle are triggered in directors' minds and emotions. For instance, as a directee shares her story of sexual abuse and strives to bring this experience to God, the director may recall her own abuse as a child. The director already may be attending therapy sessions and processing her own painful memories. However, the feelings that are created as a result of a given direction situation need to be processed in supervision also. In this way the director's abusive experience will not become a hindrance to the directee's deeper sharing. Rather it will lead to a more empathetic stance, encouraging the directee to stay with the abusive experience in her prayer.

Through supervision spiritual directors also gain deeper insight into their own relationship with and experience of God and how this relationship affects the spiritual direction process. When spiritual directors remember a particular experience of God as a result of a directee's story, they can receive great benefits from savoring it again not only during their own spiritual direction but also during supervision. The deeper the awareness of God in their own experience, the more deeply aware of God they become in their directees' experiences.

Supervision can also help directors become more aware of God's affective presence or felt absence during direction sessions. That is, they can learn to sift out the differences in the atmosphere of a direction session when God is consciously brought into a session and when God is not. This deepening awareness enables directors to remember to call on God before and during direction sessions and to pray for their directees.

Through ongoing supervision spiritual directors become more keenly aware of their own patterns of resistance, which will help them to understand and explore more deeply their directees' struggle to be open. Learning more about their areas of strength and weakness as spiritual directors reveals how their own resistant patterns affect particular directing situations.

The following diagram summarizes how supervision can be a personal and experiential learning situation for spiritual directors.

Personal Learning Experience

Personal learnings	Effects on directing situations
Growing knowledge of self	More genuine and empathetic with directees
Deepening awareness of one's own brokenness and vulnerable issues	Greater capacity to stay with directees' brokenness and unresolved issues
Deepening insight into one's own relationship with God	Greater ability to help directees savor experiences of God and recognize relational growth
Awareness of how God's affective presence or absence affects direction sessions	More readily able to call on God before and during direction sessions; more aware of God's specific presence during sessions

Growing understanding of one's own areas of resistance toward God and one's authentic self	Deeper insight into directees' resistance; greater freedom to explore it
Knowledge of growing edges and areas of strength as spiritual directors	Greater awareness of how growing edges affect particular direction situations and how strengths foster directees' spiritual growth

A Learning Experience about Spiritual Growth and Human Issues

Through the process of supervision spiritual directors also gain an experiential understanding of religious experience and spiritual growth and the significant issues that affect their directees' lives. By preparing verbatims and processing their own experience in supervision, spiritual directors indirectly learn about God's ways. Thus their theoretical knowledge about religious experience turns into experiential insights. They are able to identify key dynamics of experiencing God and spiritual growth. These dynamics include God's initiative and desire, human longing for God, patterns of movement and countermovement, the process of purification, obstacles to experiencing God's love, and growth in intimacy and mutuality with God. The uniqueness and beauty of each directee's experience of God unfolds during direction sessions. Consequently, the "teachable moments" when a spiritual or theological truth is clarified in supervision allow for a deeper understanding of God's movement. A beautiful tapestry of religious experience is woven into directors' experiential understanding.

Spiritual directors also learn a great deal about significant issues that affect people's lives, such as addiction, codependency, family dysfunctions, childhood abuse and neglect, midlife transition, and the grieving process. Spiritual directors learn much theory about these pertinent matters through workshops, courses, and reading but especially during supervision, where they can process their own reactions and thus learn a great deal about the issues themselves and the best way to handle them. For instance, during supervision a novice spiritual director explores personal anxieties resulting from a directee's sexual abuse as a child. The director learns how to address childhood abuse by processing personal feelings and verbal responses. At a given "teachable moment," the supervisor may offer specific guidelines of how best to deal with sexual abuse in spiritual direction and, in particular, with this directee.

Or a directee may come to grips with food addiction. The director, who also has a compulsive attitude toward food, initially avoids the issue during supervision. However, by becoming aware of this tendency, the director begins a process of self-examination. Working through personal attitudes toward food addiction as well as the director's addictiveness enables the director to learn about the dynamics involved.

Deeper Understanding
of the Process of Spiritual Direction

Through supervision spiritual directors not only learn about themselves and their directees but also discover a great deal about the process and skills of spiritual direction. This learning experience occurs in three ways: through *modeling*, through *role-playing*, and through *teachable moments*. First, supervisors model the contemplative approach to spiritual direction by the contemplative and evocative stance they assume in supervision. They become mentors, demonstrating to directors how to draw water from the well of interior experience. The same skills of listening, savoring, exploring, and offering feedback are used in both supervision and spiritual direction even though the content is different. During supervision the well encompasses the interior experience of the spiritual director while directing; in spiritual direction the well contains the directee's experience of God and life. Spiritual directors, then, experience and learn the skills and process of spiritual direction through their supervisors' approach.

Second, spiritual directors learn a great deal about spiritual direction by role-playing during supervision. After spiritual directors explore the reasons their verbal responses diverge from directees' experiences, supervisors can help them, through role-playing, savor these experiences. To practice savoring skills during supervision enables directors to apply these same skills in various directing situations.

Third, during supervision teachable moments may emerge that are related to specific dynamics of spiritual direction, such as helping directees to share their negative feelings with God or to bring out into the open an unresolved issue that has been hidden in the directee's consciousness. Supervisors may offer suggestions about how to work with either dynamic, but only after the director's interior experience has been explored in-depth.

Thus supervision and spiritual direction processes are the same in significant ways. Their similarity enables spiritual directors to assimilate spiritual direction skills through the supervision process. The following is a summary of the similarities and differences between these two processes.

Similarities

Supervision	Spiritual direction

Focus:
    experience, not theory
    or ideas
	Focus:
	    experience, not theory
	    or ideas

Contemplative:
    attentiveness to what is
	Contemplative:
	    attentiveness to what is

Aware of God's presence:
    during direction and
    supervision sessions
	Aware of God's presence:
	    in person's experience and
	    during direction session

Evocative, rather than didactic: drawing water from the well	Evocative, rather than didactic: drawing water from the well

Suggestions for reflection
and prayer

Suggestions for reflection
and prayer

Differences

Supervision

Spiritual direction

Director's inner experience
  while directing
  —Reactions
  —Reasons
  —Results

Directee's experience of life
  and God
  —Recognizing
  —Savoring
  —Responding

Feedback:
  underscore interior movements and growing edges
  in director

Feedback:
  underscore interior movements in directee

Role-play is used to help a
  director learn a particular
  direction skill

A Learning Experience for Supervisors

Although some courses and workshops are being offered on supervision around the country, most supervisors have learned their ministry through actual experience. By reflecting on their experience on their own and with others, supervisors can learn a great deal about the purposes, content, focus, process, and skills of supervision. They learn ways to develop a discerning heart and to skillfully and reverently delve into their supervisees' experience. Further, through the actual experience of supervision, they gain a clearer understanding of the differences between supervision and consultation. The following diagram is a succinct description of these differences.

Differences between
Supervision and Consultation

Supervision	Consultation
Focus is on spiritual director	Focus is on directee
Focus is on interior life of director while directing	Focus is on interior movements of directee
Focus is on areas of unfreedom, resistance, blind spots, unresolved issues, and life experiences affecting the director as director	Focus is on struggle, vulnerability, issues, life experiences, pain of the directee
The content consists of the director's experience of God, particularly while directing, and its effects on directing situations	The content consists of the directee's experience of God
Verbatim: Focus is on the responses of the director	Verbatim: Focus is on the directee's sharing
Begins with spiritual director and returns to directee and directing situation for applications, for example:	Begins, stays, and ends with focus on the directee

> Having noticed (name the awareness), how might you respond to the directee now?
> Having explored these interior movements (name the movements), how do you feel toward Joan?
> How does this new insight (named by supervisor) affect your presence with Bill?

Although most of the time in a supervision session is spent on the experience of the spiritual director as director, sometimes a beginning director will need to consult about a particular issue of the directee, such as sexual orientation or the loss of a loved one. Consultation should take place at the *end* of the supervision session *after* directors have explored at length their own inner experience. For example, in a two-hour supervision session the supervisor and director may agree to spend the last twenty minutes for consultation on a particular issue. It is important that the supervisor and director are clear about the distinction and are able to identify when they are moving from supervision to consultation.

One of the greatest challenges of supervision is to maintain focus on the inner life of the director—not on the directee's experiences. The following guidelines may help maintain the proper focus.

- Be sure both the spiritual director and the supervisor are clear about the focus of supervision.

- If either the supervisor or the director notices that the session is moving to consultation, call it to the other's attention and bring the focus back to the director's experience.

- State a given time for consultation (when it is needed, such as the last fifteen minutes of the session), or set up another time altogether.

- Periodically evaluate the supervision sessions with a special emphasis on focus and content.

- Suggest other ways that a director can gain information on a given issue, such as through a book, an article, or a workshop.

Conclusion

As the supervisor, Jesus, and the spiritual director gaze into the well of the director's inner experience while directing, the director learns a great deal about him- or herself as a person and as a director. The spiritual director gains many experiential insights about religious experience, directees, life issues, and the process and skills of spiritual direction. At the same time, supervisors learn specific dynamics related to the purposes, focus, process, and skills of supervision. Theoretical knowledge is transformed into the richness of experiential learning. Supervision, then, becomes a life-giving environment where directors and supervisors experience an "intimate knowledge and relish[ing] of the truth" of God's ways in themselves and in others.

Questions for Reflection and Discussion

For Supervisors

1. What specific realities are your supervisees learning about themselves? their directees? God?

2. Describe several "teachable moments" during supervision in which you spent time giving input on a particular topic. Did these interfere or enhance the exploratory, discovery process? When seems to be the best time to offer a limited amount of input about an issue?

3. During supervision sessions, in what ways do you model a contemplative and evocative approach?

4. What are some significant insights that you have gained about the purposes, content, process, and skills of supervision?

5. What have you learned about the differences between supervision and consultation from your experience of supervision? What has helped you to maintain the proper focus?

For Spiritual Directors

1. Through supervision, what significant insights have you gained about yourself as a person? What have you

learned about your patterns of resistance? religious experience? spiritual direction? or specific issues?

2. Describe one or two moments in supervision when you felt like you were in spiritual direction. What precipitated the experience? How was it different from spiritual direction?

3. In what ways has your supervisor modeled a contemplative and evocative approach to spiritual direction?

4. Describe one or two "teachable moments" when your supervisor shared some input or made suggestions about a particular issue. Did those moments interfere with or enhance the exploratory approach?

5. Describe one or two moments when the supervision process moved to consultation. How did that happen? Did you and/or your supervisor become aware of the shift? If so, what did both of you do to bring the focus back to your experience?

A Contemplative Moment

Long ago Solomon asked God for an understanding heart: "O Lord, give your servant an understanding heart to guide your people" (1 Kgs 3:9a). In your ministry of spiritual direction and supervision, discover the specific ways and with whom you need this gift. Ask God for what you need.

See God form an understanding heart within you, as a potter forms clay, molding it to fit your body, mind, spirit, and experience. Visualize what your understanding heart might look like. Experience what it feels like. Envision God infusing spiritual knowledge and wisdom into your heart and mind.

Contemplate these words from the Book of Wisdom and relate them to your understanding heart and to your ministry:

Within her is a spirit intelligent, holy, unique,
manifold, subtle, active, incisive, unsullied,
lucid, invulnerable, benevolent, sharp, irresistible,
beneficent, loving to humanity, steadfast,

dependable, unperturbed, almighty, all-seeing,
penetrating all intelligent,
pure and most subtle spirits;
for Wisdom is quicker to move than any motion;
she is so pure, she pervades and permeates all things.
She is an aura of the power of God,
pure emanation of the glory of the Almighty;
hence nothing impure can find a way into her.
She is a reflection of the eternal light,
untarnished mirror of God's active power,
image of God's goodness. (Wis 7:22–26)

Prayer for an Understanding Heart

God, my constant companion and teacher, I ask you for the gift of an understanding heart. Give me, I beseech you, an intimate knowledge of myself, of you, and of your ways in others.

Help me to bask in the truth of who I am in you, who others are in you.

Teach me the truths of everlasting life, so that I can help others discover these truths.

You revealed long ago that your ways are not our ways, nor are your thoughts our thoughts (Is 55:8). Let your mysterious ways and transformative thoughts seep into my mind and heart, so I can journey with others as you reveal your ways and thoughts to them.

I ask for a deeper understanding of and insight into your loving heart and magnificent mind, so I can walk with others in wisdom and true knowledge.

"Direct me in your ways, O God, and teach me your paths; guide me in your truth" (Ps 25:4–5a).

Conclusion

Supervision helps spiritual directors to look deeply into the well of their interior life as spiritual directors and as persons. This contemplative and evocative process enables hidden feelings and areas of unfreedom to come into the light. The more keenly spiritual directors notice their own interior movements, feel their own feelings, become aware of their areas of unfreedom and struggle, and savor their experiences of God, the more freely they will be able to offer these gifts to their directees.

Each supervision experience of insight and freedom has a rippling effect. As spiritual directors grow more aware of hidden feelings and process unresolved issues, they become freer to stay with directees during direction sessions. The water of God's life-giving presence permeates the spiritual direction experience more completely. Both directee and director become like sponges absorbing living water.

On the following page is a diagram of Jesus, the supervisor, and the spiritual director looking into the well of the spiritual director's interior life. This illustration visually summarizes the purposes, process, and skills of supervision. A spiritual director's prayer and a supervisor's prayer follow the diagram.

Looking into the Well

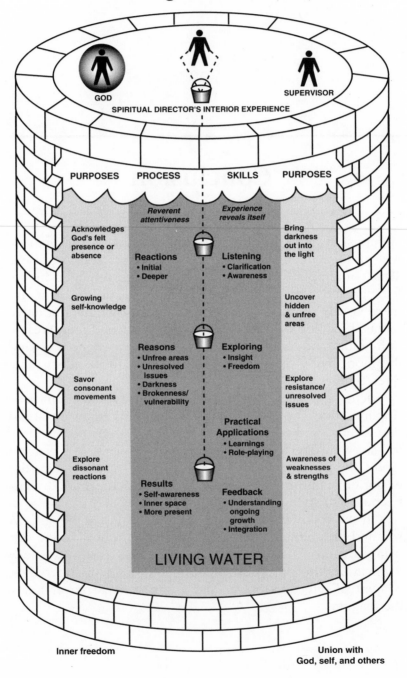

GOD

SUPERVISOR

SPIRITUAL DIRECTOR'S INTERIOR EXPERIENCE

| PURPOSES | PROCESS | SKILLS | PURPOSES |

Reverent attentiveness *Experience reveals itself*

Acknowledges God's felt presence or absence

Reactions
• Initial
• Deeper

Listening
• Clarification
• Awareness

Bring darkness out into the light

Growing self-knowledge

Reasons
• Unfree areas
• Unresolved issues
• Darkness
• Brokenness/ vulnerability

Exploring
• Insight
• Freedom

Uncover hidden & unfree areas

Savor consonant movements

Explore resistance/ unresolved issues

Practical Applications
• Learnings
• Role-playing

Explore dissonant reactions

Awareness of weaknesses & strengths

Results
• Self-awareness
• Inner space
• More present

Feedback
• Understanding ongoing growth
• Integration

LIVING WATER

Inner freedom

Union with God, self, and others

Spiritual Director's Prayer

God of the well, thank you for the waters of life that you offer to refresh and renew me.

God of my inner well, thank you for the living waters of your love that I soak in each day.

Thank you for the peaceful water of your serenity that I can enter into in time of turmoil.

Thank you for the clear water of your Spirit from which I can receive your gift of discernment.

When I am with someone during the sacred hour of spiritual direction, help me to be aware of the deep well of your holy presence. May your sparkling, refreshing water of love flow over this person and over me, a privileged companion of your love.

May the clear, pure waters of grace permeate my mind, heart, and spirit so that I can be a discerning companion and a contemplative presence.

Enlighten the well within me so that I can see blind spots and darkness that may prevent me from flowing with your Spirit.

Help me to be gentle with my own brokenness as well as my directee's. Help me to embrace my areas of struggle rather than avoid them, because in my self-embracing stance I will grow freer to embrace others' struggles and darkness.

Help me to be a healer of others' wounds because I am letting you heal my wounds.

Let the well of my interior life be open and free so that my directees know that in this holy moment of spiritual direction they can be open, vulnerable, and free to be themselves.

I ask that this time be holy time—time that my directees can let the living waters of your love flow over the darkness of their life and spirit and flow into the empty spaces of their heart.

Supervisor's Prayer

Companion God, I ask you for the gift of a companioning heart like yours. Help me empathetically journey with the spiritual directors that you have entrusted to my care. I ask for the grace of constant awareness of your presence during supervision sessions.

Give me the heart of Jesus as he stood with the woman at the well, gazing into the well of her interior life and nurturing her with the living waters of divine love.

Use my reverent presence and gentle proddings to open up areas of darkness and unfreedom in these spiritual directors. Help them to lower the bucket into their interior space of direction experiences and to find those that need knowledge, discernment, strength, and freedom.

As we contemplate together their inner space during this sacred time of supervision, give us discerning hearts and minds.

When resistance predominates, give these directors the strength to explore what is underneath their resistance; give me a steadfast heart to stay with them.

When blindness pervades, give them your sight and insight; surround us with the light of your wisdom.

When feelings of inadequacy persist, give them your confidence; help me to be an encouraging companion.

When wounded and broken areas emerge, surround them with your healing embrace; fill me with your compassionate love.

When anxiety and fear linger, give them your courage; give me an understanding heart.

God of light, I ask for the gift of a discerning heart in order to know where to move and when to stay with certain experiences; for the courage to go deeper into their interior well; and for the freedom to stay with their weaknesses, vulnerability, and brokenness.

God of darkness, help me walk with spiritual directors in their darkness so that they can move into the light of self-knowledge and spiritual insight.

God of the well, drench me with the living waters of your love so I can be a loving presence to others.

Thank you, companion God, for the privilege of journeying with others as they grow in knowledge of your ways in themselves and in others.

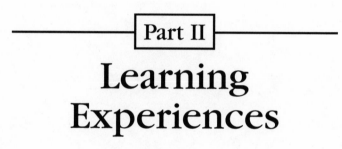

Part II
Learning
Experiences

Learning Experiences:
An Overview

The learning experiences described in the following pages are practical exercises for individuals and groups to reflect on their experience of spiritual direction and supervision. They are concrete ways to deepen one's understanding of the purposes and process of supervision. They also provide opportunities to practice supervision skills.

There are two sets of learning experiences. The first set, learning experiences 1–15, is intended for reflection and discussion by all three groups: spiritual directors, supervisors who are not offering supervision in the context of a training program, and supervisors who are doing supervision as part of a formal program. The second set, learning experiences 16–21, is intended for supervisors and educators conducting a training program for spiritual directors.

These learning experiences offer opportunities to integrate the theory and principles of supervision into one's experience of spiritual direction and supervision.

Learning Experiences 1–15: For Spiritual Directors, Supervisors, and Developmental Programs

Learning Experience 1

Spiritual Direction Log

Spiritual directors may use a log to reflect on their sessions and discernment of interior movements. For each session a director may (1) write a verbatim of the conversation or (2) describe the person's experience in phrases and sentences without writing a complete verbatim. This log is especially helpful for spiritual directors in training programs.

Directions: For ongoing spiritual direction, directed retreats, and the Nineteenth Annotation retreat from the *Spiritual Exercises,* keep a log of each direction session with the conversation between the director and directee in the right-hand column and their reactions in the left-hand column. The director writes down impressions—words and phrases—that describe the feelings and interior movements occurring within him- or herself. Each session should include the following:

Pseudonym of directee:

Date of session:

Duration of session:

Director's reactions   **Conversation**

(This section is usually one or two pages.)

Directee's movements/countermovements:

Director's movements/countermovements:

The affective experience of God's presence (describe):

Reflections on the session:

Questions for Reflection and Discussion

1. How does a spiritual direction log assist individual growth as spiritual directors? Be specific, and give examples.

2. What are the long-term benefits of a spiritual direction log?

3. How does a spiritual direction log help the supervision process?

Learning Experience 2

Discernment in the Spiritual Director

Learning experience 2 consists of two parts. Part I, an outline describing interior movements in the spiritual director, serves primarily as a reflection tool to help spiritual directors develop a discerning heart and illuminate the content of supervision. Part II offers a way to help spiritual directors pray with spiritual direction experiences. Both parts can assist spiritual directors in the process of self-supervision and help them to decide what to bring to individual or peer group supervision.

Part I: The Experience of Interior Movements

1. What do spiritual directors experience in spiritual direction sessions?

   a) God's presence for their directees and themselves

   b) Interior reactions to God's presence:

      (1) Harmony with directee and God

      (2) Dissonance with directee and God

   c) Resistance, struggle, repression, denial

     d) Dynamics of relationship, such as transference, coun-
     tertransference, projection

2. Why do spiritual directors experience movement toward God in direction sessions?

     a) In prayerful dialogue with God themselves

     b) In touch with their own feelings in prayer

     c) God's felt presence in direction sessions

     d) Director facilitates dialogue between God and directee

     e) Moved, touched by directee's experience of God

3. How do spiritual directors experience movement toward God in direction sessions?

     a) Affective sense of God's presence

     b) A felt union with a directee and God

     c) A feeling of congruence, peace, joy, life, fullness, freedom, serenity

     d) A guiding presence of the Spirit

4. Why do spiritual directors experience resistance or countermovement in direction sessions?

     a) Mirroring or reacting to a directee's resistance

     b) An unresolved issue in the director

     c) A lack of freedom in a particular area of one's life

     d) Countertransference—a directee reminds the director of a significant person whom he or she is struggling with, either consciously or unconsciously

5. How do spiritual directors experience resistance/counter-movement in direction sessions?

   a) Boredom, restlessness, distractions, difficulty listening to the directee

   b) Movement away from a contemplative presence with a person to chattiness, preachiness, teaching, advice giving or problem solving

   c) Feeling of being unfocused or lost (how did we get here? where are we going? what are we doing?)

   d) Not feeling God's presence (where did you go, God?)

   e) Feelings of avoidance before a session

6. What processes can help directors to be more in touch with their interior reactions?

   a) Sensitive and consistent self-awareness through self, individual and group supervision

   b) Frequently asking themselves: What are my feelings? What are my fears and hopes? What are my struggles? What are my joys? What need is alive at this moment? Whose need is it?

   c) Continuous working through issues, struggles, resistances

   d) Prayer before, during, and after direction sessions:

      (1) For gift of self-awareness

      (2) For gift of sensitivity and openness to the "spirits"—their spirit, directee's spirit, God's Spirit

   e) Individual spiritual direction (and counseling when needed)

7. What is the result of spiritual directors being self-aware and prayerful?

    a) Interior freedom from binding interior realities operating at the moment

    b) Inner space to receive and move with a directee's experiences of God

    c) Freedom to explore deeply the resistance and countermovement of directees

    d) Clear sense of direction and timing in a directee's experience; what to focus on and when

Part II: Sifting through Interior Movements: Praying with Spiritual Direction Experiences

Go to the well of your spiritual direction experiences. Ask God to be with you at the well. As you gaze into the well notice the life-giving water of God's constant presence.

Contemplate each spiritual direction experience of the current week, possibly using your log. As you sit with each experience, prayerfully reflect, jotting down responses. You may even want to draw a well on a sheet of paper and write down your reflections.

Be attentive to your own interior movements before, during, and after the session. Identify some of these reactions and movements. Was the session mostly one of consolation or desolation?

What was the strongest movement? Was it one of consolation—movement toward God? Or was it desolation—feeling distant from God or movement away from God? Either way, describe the movement.

Describe God's felt presence or felt absence during the session. Which was stronger: God's felt presence or God's felt absence?

Reflect on your own presence during the session. Was it contemplative? evocative? focused? companioning? discerning?

free? caring? patient? Or was your presence unfocused? frag-
mented? aggressive? unfree? self-absorbed? impatient? talkative?
Did it lead to a problem-solving or advice-giving approach? If
so, do you know what moved you into this stance?

Did any of your own issues emerge during the session? If
so, were they present in a congruent way in that the particular
issue or issues did not interfere with your staying with the
directee? Did they help you feel empathy or compassion, or
did your own emerging issue(s) interfere with the session? Did
it distract your attention from what the directee was sharing?

Be with God with all these considerations, and share with
God any feelings that come to you now. Be attentive to God's
response and presence with you. Let yourself and your
directee be drenched with the living waters of God's love.

Learning Experience 3

Direction Experiences to Bring to Supervision

Learning experience 3 outlines the types of direction experiences that spiritual directors bring to supervision and gives examples of each. Spiritual directors preparing for supervision may find this outline a helpful reflection tool for deciding which situation to present.

The Experience of Interior Movements

Movement Evokes Movement

Consolation/movement occurs in both the directee and the director.

- A director wants help in staying with the directee's experience of God and needs assistance in being contemplative so that the directee can unfold the richness of the experience.

- The director wants assistance in honing contemplative skills; that is, the ability to help a directee linger longer with a particular experience of God.

Movement Evokes Countermovement

The directee is in consolation but the director is in resistance/countermovement.

- A directee shares an intimate experience of God, and the director becomes emotionally distant.

- A directee shares an overwhelming experience of God's love, and the director feels envy and resentment.

Countermovement Evokes Movement

The directee is in resistance and the director is in consolation.

- A directee is avoiding God in prayer because of a painful loss, and the director is patient and accepting of the directee's resistance.

- A directee says, "nothing happened in my prayer this month," and the director calmly asks God to be present as the "nothingness" is explored.

Countermovement Evokes Countermovement

Resistance in the directee causes desolation in the spiritual director.

- A directee is not praying, and the director is frustrated.

- A directee is being superficial (avoiding deep feelings), and the director is bored and distracted.

The Spiritual Director's Personal Issues

Areas of Unfreedom, Vulnerability, and/or Brokenness

A directee's sharing of his or her experience opens up an area of unfreedom in the director, produces a feeling of vulnerability, or evokes the shadow side of the director.

- A directee talks continuously, which produces feelings in the director of being unimportant and unnecessary.

- A directee, though prayerful and in touch with God, does not pray at a regular time each day, which stirs the director's perfectionism and need for order.

Mirroring Dynamic

The director is struggling with a similar situation as the directee.

- Loss of a significant other through death.

- Struggle to be intimate or vulnerable.

- An addiction.

Moral, Theological, Spiritual, and Cultural Differences

The director experiences inner conflict because of a significant moral, theological, spiritual, or cultural difference.

- A directee rationalizes an immoral action, and the director experiences pain and anger.

- A director struggles with a directee's feminine image of and approach to God.

- A director struggles with a directee's lack of awareness regarding important social issues.

A Contemplative Attitude and Approach

A director may need to explore experiences that are directly related to the process and approach of spiritual direction.

Lacking a Contemplative Attitude and Atmosphere

- God's presence is not attended to or felt during direction sessions.

- A director realizes that he or she is talking too much or trying too hard with a certain directee.

Weaknesses As a Spiritual Director

- A director finds it difficult to listen from the heart; too much "head" work.

- A previously undisclosed experience is revealed (such as periodic bouts of depression), and the director feels uncomfortable or inadequate.

A Significant Breakthrough

- After months of slipping into a teaching role during direction sessions, a director finally feels what it is like to be evocative.

- A director who has had a heady approach to spiritual direction realizes the benefits of helping a directee focus on feelings and affective experiences of God rather than focusing on thoughts and beliefs about God.

Relationship between Director and Directee

A Struggle in the Director-Directee Relationship

- Strong negative or positive feelings in director or directee.

- Feeling controlled or being too controlling.

Issues of Transference and Countertransference

- A directee projects a negative mother image onto the director and becomes fearful of sharing during direction sessions.

- The director feels unexplained anger toward a directee.

A Painful Termination of a Direction Relationship

- A directee unexpectedly ends a long-term direction relationship.

- While working through strong transference issues, a directee abruptly decides to stop coming for spiritual direction.

Praying with Difficult Direction Experiences

Because spiritual direction is a trinitarian experience—that is, God, the directee, and the director are in communion with one another—it is vital that spiritual directors take the time to pray with their direction experiences, particularly difficult or challenging ones. Praying about such experiences can contribute to spiritual directors' growing insight and inner freedom as well as assist them in preparing for supervision. Learning experience 4 describes this method of prayer.

Praying with a Difficult Direction Experience

To prepare for supervision, take some quality prayer time with a difficult direction experience that you would like to bring to supervision. You may also want to pray with other challenging experiences that you are not bringing to supervision. The following contemplation can assist your prayer. You may want to prepare a written review after your prayer time is completed.

A Contemplation: Looking into the Well

Go to the well of your direction experiences. Look into the well of your interior experience while directing. Bring your awareness, your heart, and yourself into God's loving presence. Notice that God is with you at the well, gazing into it with you.

As you sit in God's presence at the well, let a particular direction experience come to mind. Ask God to remind you of an experience in which you were struggling or resistant or about which you had some strong feelings during or after the session.

Remember the experience. Visualize it. Relive it. See the directee. Feel the struggle or resistance again. Experience your feelings again. Let this direction experience and your feelings arise within yourself, slowly and reverently. Be aware of God's presence now as you remember and relive.

What are your feelings? Identify them specifically. What is your struggle? Identify it concretely. What is the underlying reason(s) for your reactions? your struggles?

Bring to mind any unresolved issue or vulnerable area within you that was being touched or stirred through this direction experience. What was that issue or area? How do you feel now as you contemplate this area with God?

What was God's presence, or lack of felt presence, like during the direction session? What is God's presence like now as you pray with this experience?

Share with God the feelings, struggles, and reasons for your reactions. Be attentive to God's response. Ask God for what you need for your own growth to help this directee and direction situation. Let the living water of God's love permeate you, your directee, and the situation. Thank God for God's loving presence with you.

Write down what happened as you contemplated this experience. What was God's presence like? What was your directee like? What happened in you as a result of this contemplation? Did any new insights arise?

Questions for Reflection and Discussion for Supervisors and Spiritual Directors

1. Using a contemplative mode, ask yourself what specific benefits result from praying with spiritual direction experiences.

2. How can praying with difficult direction experiences help the supervision experience?

3. Describe one or two experiences of praying with a difficult direction situation. What changes took place in you and your directee as a result of your prayer?

Verbatim Case Study

Suggested Verbatim Form

Many developmental programs for spiritual directors use verbatims of a specific direction conversation as a springboard for supervision. A helpful format is a two-column verbatim in which spiritual directors write down their felt reactions in the left column and key words or phrases of the conversation on the ride side. The left column helps spiritual directors to be specifically aware of their own interior movements while directing. The right side assists directors in noticing more concretely when they move away from their directees' experiences and when they stay with them in their verbal responses.

1. **Factual information:** Your name, directee's pseudonym, date of session, number of meetings, date, and number of supervision meeting.

2. **Background of directee:** A few sentences on information helpful to understanding this session and/or sessions to this point. For example, Mary has been in resistance during our last two sessions; Ryan is beginning to pray in an affective and relational way; Joan is struggling in her relationship with her husband; Amy has been working through the loss of a significant relationship; Bill's concept

of God is changing from the image of a distant father to a supportive brother.

3. **A key part of the conversation**

    a) *Focus:* a part of the conversation where you as direc-
        tor experience strong negative feelings (anger, frus-
        tration, fear, inadequacy, resistance, confusion) or
        positive feelings (joy, pleasure, delight because of
        God's presence). Supervision focuses primarily on
        those reactions and feelings in which you moved
        away emotionally from the directee, God, or yourself.

    b) *Format:*

        (1) After the direction session (not during) write
            down or tape-record as much of the conversation
            as possible.

        (2) Jot down in the right-hand column a two-page
            account of a key part of the conversation.

        (3) Write down in the left column your interior reac-
            tions next to as many responses as possible.

    c) *Example:*

Director's Reactions	Conversation
Calm, patient	Director 1: This experience came from deep within.
	Ann 1: Yes, deep within me. It was the story of Jesus healing the leper. I saw the leper standing there (waves her
Repulsion	arms to show me where). His sores were ugly and I could smell the stench (describes the leper further). I
Anxiety	saw Jesus coming toward the leper.

His face lit up, and he moved forward and embraced him! That surprised me.

Surprised me, too!

D2:   Jesus embraced the leper and that surprised you.

A2:   Yes, and embarrassed me.

D3:   Embarrassed you?

Moved by her honesty

A3:   Yes. I hold people off, and I keep them from coming too close.

D4:   You hold people off.

Uneasy

A4:   People come to me, but I hold them off sometimes because of the way they are, the way they look. (They explore this for a few moments.)

D5:   Going back to when you first saw the leper, how did you feel?

Surprised at her honesty

A5:   Oh, I was the leper too (teary-eyed). My own self-centeredness was my disease. But Jesus embraced me.

Uncomfortable

D6:   Jesus embraced you too in your self-centeredness.

The conversation would be written in this fashion for about another page or so.

4.   **Director's experience**

- Where do you experience the strongest feeling? What is it? Do you know what is underlying this feeling?

- Where/how are you as director moving toward or away from God? the directee's experience?

- How would you describe God's presence during the session? Be as specific and descriptive as possible.

- Why are you using this session or session portion? What do you want your supervisor to help you focus on? unpack? explore? savor?

5. **Directee's experience**

   - How would you describe the directee's personal relationship with God and affective experience of God? Where/how is this person moving toward and away from God?

   - What life issues is the directee dealing with? How are these issues affecting the person's experience of God? prayer life? relationship with self, others, the world?

6. **Experiential learnings**

   - What experiential learnings have you gained or were reaffirmed about God? spiritual direction? religious experience? spiritual growth? life experience? yourself as a director or as a person?

7. *Spiritual Exercises* **and Rules for Discernment (optional)**

   - Do any of the dynamics of the Weeks of the *Spiritual Exercises* apply to the directee's experience? to your experience of directing? Specifically name one or two of these experiences with concrete examples.

   - Do any of the Rules for Discernment apply to the directee's experience or your experience of directing? Specifically name one or two of these with concrete examples.

Questions for Reflection and Discussion

For Supervisors and Spiritual Directors

1. What are the advantages and disadvantages of using verbatims for supervision? In what other ways could a written description be presented and used for supervision?

2. Name three or four specific reasons the left column containing the spiritual director's felt reactions can be helpful for self-reflection and supervision.

3. Why is the "director's experience" section important? Would you add any questions to this section?

4. In what ways can the "directee's experience" section be helpful? the "experiential learnings" section?

Learning Experience 6
Two Examples of Verbatim Case Studies

The two case studies in this section are examples of the verbatim case study described in learning experience 5. The first case study describes a spiritual direction session in which both the directee and the director are experiencing resistance and struggle to stay with God and their deeper selves. The second study describes a direction session in which both the director and the directee are experiencing consolation.

As you peruse these verbatim case studies, I encourage you to approach them with a contemplative heart, spirit, and mind. Try to read them in a stance of prayerful discernment as if you were going to supervise these directors, either individually or in a peer group. Keep in mind the following questions as you prayerfully go along.

1. What are my feelings, thoughts, and perceptions as I read each verbatim case study? What is my strongest feeling?

2. In what specific ways can I help these directors to explore and savor their experience while directing? How can I help them understand their reasons for using the verbatim?

3. What do I hope to accomplish during the supervision session? Where is a helpful starting point?

First Verbatim Case Study: An Experience of Struggle

1. **Factual Information**
   Name of director:
   Directee's pseudonym: Suzanne
   Date of direction session:
   Date of supervision session:

2. **Background of Directee**

   Suzanne is a forty-five-year-old married woman with young adult children. She has worked in the health field most of her adult life. She is intelligent, capable, and articulate. She has been working on her relationship with God for ten years and has been in spiritual direction for more than three years. Suzanne values her relationship with God highly, but it does not bring her much consolation. She used to receive spiritual benefit from quiet, meditative time with God each morning. For many months her sense of God has been that of an aloof yet supportive figure who wants her to believe more in herself.

3. **Key Part of Conversation**

Director's Reactions	Conversation
	Director 1: So what's God been like for you lately?
	Suzanne 1: (Reflective) Hmmm . . . present.
	D2: Present.
	S2: Yeah, present.
	D3: Present? In what way?
Mildly interested; this is the way it's been for a while.	S3: Well, supportive. God continues to be saying, "Trust yourself, believe in yourself." God is standing to one side, not involved, continuing to want me to stand by myself. It's working. I'm learning to do it. It's hard, though. Scary.

D4: So that's how God has been with you lately—continuing to encourage you to believe in yourself—trust yourself. What's God like there?

Still mildly interested

(Off-handedly) Not doing much. Not saying much. Just there, in the background, wanting me to learn to trust myself. . . . And I do, more and more, but it's tough.

D5: What is?

I've heard this before but patient and "with her."

S5: Going it alone. Not using all the traditional ways I've always used in feeling my relationship with God. I got a lot out of my daily devotions to the saints and saying the rosary. But every time I think of saying the rosary and going back to my novenas, I get this strong sense inside me that these are not the right ways for me to pray right now. And I follow that. . . . (Reflecting) But I think, "Is this right? Am I doing the right thing?" Same thing with my meditations. I still am not drawn to my old meditation time in the morning. I just feel like I shouldn't have to be forcing myself to do anything, including praying.

D6: So on the one hand, you sometimes miss your old familiar ways of relating to God, but on the other hand, they just don't seem right to you at this time. Is that what you're saying?

S6: Yes.

D7: And how is God with this?

Moving from patience to tolerance

S7: Fine, I think. Yes, I know God is saying, "Go with what you think is right." I'm always checking things out with God. Constantly. I never do anything without first checking it out. (Looking off to side, reflectively.) But it's very lonely. And I'm tired.

D8: You're tired?

S8: Yes.

D9: What's that about?

Getting
discouraged

S9: My marriage. Nothing's changed there. Nothing will change there. Henry's not going to change. (Staring) The kids were home this weekend, and I realized, I'm not getting anything from Interested anybody. (Becomes angry.)

D10: What do you mean?

S10: There is not one place that I'm "getting" from. Not from my marriage, not from my kids, and certainly not from work.

D11: How does that make you feel?

Disappointed
and
discouraged

S11: Angry. I saw my children in a different light this weekend. And it wasn't too pleasant. Henry and I raised them well, I will say that for us. But they're on their own now, and it's not the same. I've lost them, in a way. It makes me angry, because I gave them a lot when they were growing up. (Reflective; shakes head.) But it really wouldn't matter, if my marriage were better.

D12: What do you mean?

Understand and
agree but feel
discouraged
about direction
of session

S12: I mean, the way they are wouldn't bother me so much if my marriage were better. I wouldn't need them as much if more of my needs were met.

4. Director's Experience

This verbatim is a good example of many of our sessions: aimless, introspective, almost thinking aloud, and not a lot to grab onto. God rarely seems strongly present, and Suzanne does not seem interested in spending much time "looking at" God. Worse, nothing healthy or therapeutic comes from concentrating on her painful issues.

However, the reason I bring this situation to supervision is not for help in knowing what to do with her but because of my lack of freedom in working with her, which seems to be based on a fear of Suzanne's anger. Her anger appears when she talks about certain subjects, and it makes me uncomfortable. I don't want it directed at me. Because of my fear, I avoid discussing them. I need help in discovering what is underneath my fear of her anger. I also need to process the absence of a felt sense of God's presence so that I can discover ways to be attentive to God during the sessions.

Second Verbatim Case Study:
An Experience of Consolation

1. **Factual Information**
   Name of director:
   Directee's pseudonym: Marcia
   Date of direction session:
   Date of supervision session:

2. **Background of Directee**

   Marcia is married and has three teenage children. She has been grieving the loss of her mother, who died a year ago.

   Family relationships, which are often troublesome, seem to be a frequent topic of discussion in sessions. At other times, Marcia talks about herself, her attitudes or faults, and the ways she contributes to these difficulties. She is a perfectionist with strong opinions. In one session a good amount of time was spent talking about how she does not take care of her own needs. I encouraged her to relax in the evenings so she can sleep better and to find some solitude, which she wants badly. Although she is a faith-filled person and delights in spiritual things, she seems unable to make time for prayer and seldom has a prayer experience to share.

3. **Key Part of Conversation**

Director's Reactions	Conversation
Eager	**Director 1:** How are things going?
Pleased	**Marcia 1:** Better, I think. I've been trying to do what we talked about last time—take care of myself more. I'm taking time to relax after dinner. I prepare my own dinner nicely and enjoy it, and—it feels better. I always did whatever other people wanted. I was a very compliant person, which came from my upbringing.
Comfortable	**D2:** Now you realize that it's important to take care of your own needs, too.
	M2: Yes, that's right. Maybe that's my first responsibility.
Hopeful	**D3:** Good. I'm glad you're doing that. What about your relationship with God? How is that going?
Interested	**M3:** I've been thinking. I've always thought of God as father, and sometimes I'm afraid of him. He's like an authority figure. Maybe I need to think of God more as mother. I need someone gentle and loving right now.
	D4: God seems like an authority figure, and you're afraid of him?
Surprised	**M4:** Yes, because he sees everything I do, and he knows everything I'm thinking. Sometimes I feel he's judging me. Maybe it has something to do with the way I felt toward my own father.
	D5: Your father was an authority figure for you?
Very interested	**M5:** Oh yes. I loved him, but I was also afraid of him, of what he might say or do. I was never close to him the way I was with my mother. We were very close, my mother and I.

D6: You were very close to your mother even just before her death, I believe?

M6: Oh yes! We were very close; we shared so much. I still miss her a great deal. She was very spiritual. We could talk about God together, and it was wonderful. I really miss that. Now there isn't anyone—family or friends—with whom I can really talk about God. Sometimes I feel angry about that.

Moved

Compassionate

Perhaps I moved too quickly here

D7: Can you tell God about your anger?

M7: I don't know.

D8: You know, when people are close they can get angry with each other. If you want to get close to God, you need to tell God how you feel.

M8: (Laughs a little) Yes, that's true. My mother and I could get angry sometimes, and it didn't affect our closeness. But I could never get angry with my father.

Moving closer

D9: You really miss that closeness with your mother, don't you?

M9: Oh yes. It's over a year now since she died, but I still miss her so much. Somehow I can't seem to pray the same now as I could when she was with me. God just doesn't seem to be as close. (They explore this a bit.)

Perking up

Taking a chance

D10: Let's talk about right now for a while. Okay?

M10: Okay. Fine. (She draws a little closer.)

D11: Do you feel God here, right now?

Pleased

M11: Oh yes, definitely.

D12: What is God like? Could you say something about God?

Feeling God present, too

M12: (Pauses) God is very gentle and caring.

D13: God's gentle and caring.

	M13:	Yes . . . (Hesitates)
At ease	D14:	Suppose you just close your eyes and prayerfully pause for a while. Notice how God seems to you at this moment. (Long pause)
	M14:	God seems to be the Good Shepherd
Identifying easily		—very loving, caring, and watchful Sheep are all around him. They are
Questioning		close to him. But I am off on the fringes. I'm holding back. I don't
Curious		know if I want to get any closer. But God is looking at me, watching me.
Disappointed in myself because I moved away from God's gaze	D15:	You're holding back . . . Are you afraid?
	M15:	Yes, I'm afraid.
	D16:	What is it that you're afraid of? Do you know?
Empathy	M16:	I'm afraid I might doubt.
Trying to keep the focus on God	D17:	How does God seem to feel about that?
	M17:	God is patiently waiting, inviting, with arms open.
Disappointed— I could have helped her look at God more	D18:	Can you tell God about your fear?
	M18:	Yes, but God doesn't seem concerned about it. He just keeps looking at me.
	D19:	God keeps looking at you.
	M19:	Yes. Waiting, patiently and lovingly. Waiting for me to do something.
Taking a risk	D20:	What would it take for you to come close to God?
	M20:	A lot of trust. I don't know if I could trust that much. I trust God, but I don't know if I could trust myself.
Right there with her	D21:	It seems like a big risk to trust and move closer to God?

	M21: Yes, it does.
	D22: What would you be risking?
Understanding, empathy	M22: I'd be afraid I couldn't be faithful, that afterward I'd begin to doubt again, that I wouldn't be worthy.
Risking; am I moving too quickly?	D23: What would happen if you decided to take a risk and just move into God's arms? Could you do that?
God present Feeling him, too	M23: Yes, I'll try. (Pause) It feels warm, secure. I feel loved . . . and cared for.
	D24: Let's just stay there for a few moments, and enjoy it . . .
Comfort, joy	(They remain silent for several minutes. God seems very present, close, and loving.)
	Perhaps you may want to tell God how being close feels.
Feeling connected with her	M24: I feel so loved and safe and comforted —so warm, as if God's holding me in his arms. (They savor this movement for a while.)
Happy, grateful	D25: (Later) That was a very precious, consoling experience.
	M25: Yes, it was wonderful.
	D26: It might be helpful for you to pray again about that experience—to savor it, enjoy it more.
	M26: Yes, I would like to do that.

4. Director's Experience

I chose this verbatim for several reasons. First, because helping someone savor an experience of God is a challenge for me, so I need some help in that. I think I could have stayed longer with God in D15 and D18, but I moved away. I want to see what is underneath my moving away from God's affective presence.

Second, I chose this session because during my last supervision session we explored my difficulty with helping directees be attentive to God. My supervisor suggested that I invite the directee to look at God during the session, which I did in this session. The results were encouraging. I was delighted that the directee could notice God as Shepherd. I want to examine my own interior movements and approach.

Third, I want help in noticing God's affective presence during this direction session so I can be more aware of God's presence in other sessions.

Three Reflections
on Supervision

As explained in chapter 8, an important phase in the supervision process is prayerful reflection on the supervision session itself. Spiritual directors are encouraged to prepare a written reflection on the interior movements explored and the experiential reasons underlying them; the significant issue(s) that emerged; God's presence during the direction session; practical applications; and other such issues (see pp. 128–30). The following excerpts are the written reflections of three spiritual directors after a supervision session.

Ryan's Reflection on a Supervision Session Mirroring Dynamic

This experience turned out to be a very emotional peer group supervision session for me. My directee made a reference to all the work she does for her elderly parents, and this triggered deep feelings within me about my own elderly parents. During the supervision session it became very apparent that I have many issues to resolve. Initially I acknowledged my feelings of guilt because my busy schedule prevents quality time with my parents. Then my feelings moved into deeper emotions of sadness and mourning: I do not want to lose my parents, but time is moving very quickly and they are both getting old. In the direction session I really struggled to stay with the directee; in the supervision session I needed an even greater measure of self-discipline to keep from crying.

My supervisors carefully helped me unpack my feelings. It became obvious that I was resisting the issue of my parents and the complex feelings that surround it. I manage to keep my emotions carefully tucked away. I am afraid of bringing them out into the open, afraid of losing control and not being able to handle the situation well. I am hesitant to spend time on this issue because of the very real fear of becoming over-whelmed with my feelings of guilt, helplessness, and grief.

My supervisors asked if I could take my fears and painful feelings to God in prayer. I realized that I had never done that before. I am afraid that God will be disappointed in me. I am afraid that God will judge me harshly. My image of God surprised even me. I had always perceived God as being loving and compassionate, yet, suddenly, here was this undeniable fear of God's judgment.

During feedback a supervisor presented to me an image that appeared to her during the supervision session of Jesus kneeling beside me and looking at me with very compassion-ate eyes. Such a positive impression will help me bring this issue to God. It certainly will give me the courage to do so.

Through processing these feelings in supervision, it became clear that my directee could cope better with elderly parent issues than I. I was almost jealous of her. I need God to help me. I need a great deal of healing. If I am going to be present to people like this directee and others with similar issues to resolve and if I really want to stay with them and not interfere with their processing, I need God's healing and encouraging presence.

I am very grateful that I have a safe, trusting environment within my peer group to allow such issues to surface. I truly believe God took advantage of this session to bring such a sensitive issue to light. I am aware that it is something I need to take to my prayer and spiritual direction.

Questions for Reflection and Discussion

1. In what way and around what issue did the mirroring dynamic apply to Ryan during his direction session?

2. List how the three R's applied during the supervision session:

   Reactions   Reasons   Results

Bea's Reflection on a Supervision Session
Area of Vulnerability in the Director

The spiritual direction session I brought to supervision was one of great depth and insight for both myself and the directee. My directee, Jean, was coping with a very difficult and painful situation. I experienced being a wounded healer; that is, it was precisely because of my own struggle that I was able to feel deeply with her and to know with complete assurance that God was calling her to a new depth of healing.

My tendency—a vulnerable area within me—is to protect people from pain, which is rooted in my fear of other people's fragility as they allow themselves to feel their pain deeply and to let God reveal darkness. This fear stems from growing up with a mother who was psychologically fragile and unable to handle emotional stress. I learned how to "protect" her, to save her from feeling stress and pain and to take these emotions on myself. Exploring these negative feelings in supervision and seeing the dichotomy within me was a healing experience. On the one hand, I experience a tremendous depth of empathy and lack of fear. On the other hand, I feel protective of another person in pain and become afraid they will not be able to cope.

During part of the direction session, I felt an inner anxiety because I wanted so much to be with Jean in her pain in a supportive and compassionate way and not to move away from her pain because of a need to protect her. Because I was aware of my vulnerability, I could feel myself relaxing and becoming contemplative with her. In another part of the session I felt like I was going to explode because I could feel Jean's pain so deeply. At the same time I asked God to continue to stay close while helping me not to "protect" Jean from necessary emotions.

As my supervisor continued to help examine a verbatim from the session and my various responses, it became very clear that God answered my prayer: My tendency to protect did not interfere with Jean processing her pain. Alleluia! I rejoice and am grateful that I was able to hold someone in pain while letting go of protective tendencies. Through supervision I realized and relived the sensation of God holding me as I was present to Jean in her pain. During that moment God was a close companion and gave me the strength to stay with Jean. I continue to be moved by God's constant faithfulness as I strive to help others come to know and love our loving God.

Questions for Reflection and Discussion

1. What was Bea's area of vulnerability with which she struggled? What is the experiential reason underlying her struggle?

2. What were some felt reactions Bea had about this struggle and the reasons for them?

3. What did Bea notice about God? What difference did God's presence make in her ability to stay with her directee's pain?

Marian's Reflection on a Supervision Session
God's Transforming Power

During a directed retreat I was Sally's spiritual director. Sally had been focusing too closely on a particular situation in her life, and her obsession was causing her great pain and feelings of guilt. She had been unable to pray and felt distant from God. Immediately I experienced strong feelings of frustration and powerlessness. What could I say to help Sally stop this behavior? How could I help her to pray?

After the session, I sat in prayer with Sally's experience and my own reactions. I felt the call to let go and trust that God was at work in her. I brought to supervision both my struggle and my time of prayer. As I shared my feelings of frustration and powerlessness, I felt myself begin to relax, letting go of the need to say the right thing. As my supervisor stayed with my experience, I felt myself move away from self-absorption and anxiety to focusing on God. When my supervisor asked how I experienced God during the direction session and prayer afterward, I replied that I sensed Jesus was next to me with his hands cupped, holding "the mess." At first it was Sally's "mess": her obsession, her inability to pray, her guilt, her helplessness. Then I saw Jesus gently holding my "mess": my frustration, my powerlessness, my worry.

My supervisor's evocative stance allowed the image of Jesus to develop. I, too, held the "mess." I sensed Jesus as my mentor, my example, showing me how to be present with the "mess" in a gentle and loving way, not trying to change or manipulate it. As I sat side by side with Jesus, I could feel his strength, a strength that I could draw upon and trust time and again during any future sessions with Sally and other directees.

I was vividly aware of Jesus in my next session with Sally. As she shared her frustrations and challenges, I sensed the presence of Jesus and I was able to hold Sally's struggling experience in a gentle and loving way. I felt free of my usual desire for the retreatant to have a good experience. I accepted that the "mess" still was unresolved. Like my mentor, Jesus, I held the "mess" gently and with care.

My supervisor encouraged me to remember this experience of Jesus with my other directees. As directees come to me monthly, Jesus and I hold their painful and messy experiences in a gentle and caring way. Being with Jesus gives me much strength and freedom and the felt awareness that all my directees are truly in God's loving hands.

Questions for Reflection and Discussion

1. What differences or transformation took place in Marian because of her affective experience of God?

2. How did this experience of God affect her presence and approach in other direction sessions?

3. How did supervision deepen Marian's experience of God? Write out or role-play the way the supervision session could have unfolded in helping Marian to expand her experience of Jesus.

Learning Experience 8

Supervision Log

Often a supervisor works with a spiritual director over a significant period of time, as long as one year. In order for supervisors to follow spiritual directors' growth and their own experience during supervision, they are encouraged to keep a supervision log. This log can assume two forms: (1) writing notes on each verbatim that a spiritual director brings to supervision; and (2) recording separate notes on each supervision session. The separate notes should contain the following areas:

Supervision Log

Factual Information

Spiritual director's pseudonym:
Date of session:
Duration of session:

Spiritual Director's Experience

Type of experience brought to supervision:

Reason for bringing this experience:

Interior movements explored:

Sense of God's presence:

Personal issues explored—theological, moral, spiritual, and cultural:

Growing edges processed:

Insights emerging:

Practical applications to future direction sessions:

Supervisor's Experience

Stance as supervisor:

Skills used:

Feedback offered to spiritual director:

Interior reactions precipitated in oneself:

Personal issues triggered:

Strengths as supervisor:

Growing edges as supervisor:

Description of God's presence during supervision:

Significant learnings and insights:

Learning Experience 9

Praying with Supervision Experiences

Go to the well of your supervision experiences. Contemplate with God each supervision session, asking God to give you a discerning heart as you contemplate together. Ask God to drench you with the life-giving waters of Jesus' gracious presence and to provide insight into your gifts and concrete experience as a supervisor.

Notice the atmosphere, pace, and presence of the supervision session. Was there a contemplative atmosphere? a discerning presence? an evocative approach? a slow or fast pace? a clear focus on the director's experience? an in-depth exploration into significant movements and issues? What was God's presence like? Ask God for the necessary qualities that will enable you to be a contemplative and caring presence.

As you ponder, reflect on the spiritual director's experience of supervision. What issues emerged for the director? growing edges? resistances? struggles? joys? frustrations? Notice God's presence with the director, and ask God to continue to bless the director's ministry of spiritual direction.

Be attentive to your inner experience during the session. What feelings arose within you? struggles? joys? resistances? personal issues? growing edges? What was God's presence like for you as supervisor? Did you ask God for what you needed? Ask God to continue to be with you as you supervise.

As you contemplate and reflect, share with God any thoughts and feelings that may arise within you. Be attentive to God's presence with and response to you. Ask God to drench you and the person you are supervising with the living waters of Jesus' love and life-giving presence.

Learning Experience 10

Awareness Examen
for Supervisors

Learning to be a supervisor requires a keen self-awareness, a clear focus, and the appropriate use of supervision skills and processes. Supervisors must reflect on their experience of supervising just as spiritual directors must reflect on their experience of directing. The more aware supervisors are of their own inner experience and use of supervision skills, the more discerning they become as supervisors in helping spiritual directors' total development. The following questions serve as an awareness examen to assist supervisors' self-awareness and their use of supervision processes and skills. It is written in the first person to aid prayerful reflection.

Contemplative Presence

1. How did I create a contemplative atmosphere during the supervision session? Was this supervision experience one of reverently drawing water from the well of the spiritual director's interior directing space? If yes, in what specific ways? If no, am I aware of what the experience was like?

2. How present was I to the spiritual director's experience? Where was I listening from? my mind? my affectivity? my imagination? my interior space? a combination of these?

3. Was I aware of God's presence during the supervision session? What was the sense of God's felt presence or absence like?

Supervision Purposes, Process, and Skills

1. How would I name the situation or experience that the spiritual director brought to the session? What affective responses surfaced in the director as we explored? What issues emerged?

2. How was I present with the spiritual director's resistance? Was I reverent? contemplative? evocative? challenging? confrontative? aggressive? How do I feel about my presence and approach during the session?

3. What skills were used during the session? Could I have applied other skills?

4. Was there a difference in the affectivity of the spiritual director as the session progressed? What difference(s) did I notice?

5. Did I see or sense any growth in the director's interior freedom from the beginning to the end of the session? Concretely, what was the new freedom that emerged?

Spiritual Director's Inner Experience

1. Did the focus stay on the spiritual director's affective experience? If yes, how did this focus bear fruit?

2. If the session moved away from the spiritual director's experience, how and when did that happen? Was I aware of the movement away during the session? Did I move back to the director's experience?

3. What might I do differently next time to keep the focus on the director's experience?

Supervisor's Inner Experience

1. What affective reactions surfaced in me during the session: excitement? joy? peace? satisfaction? frustration? impatience? anxiety? fear? Do I know the reason for these reactions?

2. What happened with any negative feelings that surfaced in me? Did they prevent me from being fully present to the director? Was I able to clear a space within me in order to be fully present? If so, how did I do this? Have I taken the time to process my feelings since the session?

Significant Insights

1. What felt knowledge (felt insights) did the spiritual director gain about him- or herself as a director? as a person?

2. What insights about spiritual direction and supervision did the director gain or were reaffirmed through the supervision session?

3. What insights about supervision purposes, focus, process, and skills did I gain or have been reinforced?

Learning Experience 11
Periodic Evaluation of Supervision Experience

A spiritual director usually is supervised by one person for about a year. During that time it can be helpful for both the supervisor and the spiritual director to periodically evaluate how supervision is progressing. The following reflection questions can assist in this joint evaluation.

Questions for Reflection and Discussion

1. In general, how has supervision been proceeding? In what specific ways have the supervision sessions been helpful?

2. Has anything been unhelpful or counterproductive?

3. Has the spiritual director been bringing varied direction situations or experiences to supervision? If so, what have been the benefits? If not, why not? Would it be more helpful for the director to bring a variety of direction situations to the session?

4. Are we keeping the focus on the experience of the spiritual director while directing? If so, how can we explore even more deeply? If not, in what concrete ways can we maintain focus on the director's experience?

5. Has the approach and process been contemplative and evocative? If not, in what specific ways can we improve upon this approach?

6. What have been some of the graces and blessings of taking a contemplative and evocative approach with a clear focus on the director's experience?

7. In what ways, through supervision, is the spiritual director developing the art and skill of discerning interior movements in him- or herself and in his or her directees?

8. What have been the key issues that are emerging for the spiritual director through supervision? the growing edges? the areas of weaknesses and strengths? In what specific ways is the director working with these issues?

9. What are the significant insights that have emerged through supervision for the spiritual director about the spiritual direction process and skills? about the spiritual director as a director and as a person? about God's ways in people? about supervision?

10. How can supervision sessions be improved? What skills can be used that have not been operative? What skills can be applied more often?

Two Models
of Peer Group Supervision

Model 1: Peer Group Supervision
for Ongoing Spiritual Direction

A. Presentation of Case

    1. Information about the directee

    2. Spiritual direction conversation read aloud

    3. Several moments of prayerful reflection

    4. Questions for clarification

    5. Reason for presenting the verbatim

B. Group Exploration

    1. Core experience of supervision session

    2. Group helps director to unpack, discover, savor, and create inner space

3. Group exploration conducted in a contemplative, reverent, and evocative manner

C. **Group Prayer and Feedback**

1. Period of quiet prayer

2. Each participant shares one observation, insight, image, feeling, suggestion, or question

D. **Group Insights**

1. Significant insights about God, prayer, religious experience, life experience, spiritual growth, spiritual direction, and supervision

2. (Optional) Relationships between these insights and the *Spiritual Exercises* and Rules for Discernment

Model 2: Peer Group Supervision during Retreats

Model 2 differs from the first model in several ways: (1) it allows time for more than one director to present a direction situation; (2) usually verbal, not written, presentations are made; and (3) a presenting director moves immediately to his or her inner experience with little reference to the retreatant.

A. **Determination of Presenters**
    Participants state who needs to present during this peer group time. For instance, in a group of five, three directors may need to present on a given day.

B. **Presentation by First Director**
    The first presenter shares succinctly the inner experience or issue he or she needs to process. The group helps the presenter to unpack his or her experience in a contemplative and evocative way.

C. **Group Prayer and Feedback**
    After a moment of quiet prayer, each participant may choose to share an observation, insight, or suggestion with the presenter. Each sharing must be very succinct to allow time for the other directors.

Presentation by Second Director, Group Prayer, and Feedback

(Same principles and procedure as first director)

Presentation by Third Director, Group Prayer, and Feedback

(Same principles and procedure as first director)

Learning Experience 13

Case Studies for Role-Play and Discussion

Role-play each of the following case studies, one person being the spiritual director and the other the supervisor. Try to make your session as authentic as possible. Then reflect on the questions that follow each case study and discuss them as a group.

As you are preparing each role-play, remember the following questions:

1. What do you see happening? What type of direction situation or experience was illustrated?

2. Enter into the spiritual director's mind and heart. How might you feel? What feelings, concerns, and thoughts would you bring to supervision in order to process?

3. Do a role-play with your supervisor. Explore your feelings and thoughts and how you might handle the situation.

Case Study 1: Sister Anne's Experience

Sister Anne, a forty-six-year-old parish minister, has been offering spiritual direction for more than three years. A warm and caring person, she is well liked and appreciated.

Steve, a married man with three children, has been coming to Anne for spiritual direction for almost two years. Initially he attended sessions every other week for a period of six months but has since reduced his sessions to monthly visits.

Spiritual direction has been going well. Steve is becoming aware of his feelings, and he is relating to God in a more personal and affective way. Before beginning spiritual direction he had a rather heady approach to life, prayer, and God. Now he feels that God is a supportive friend who helps him in the daily struggles of life and work. The story of the walk to Emmaus has been significant in Steve's prayer for a while. He talks over his concerns, feelings, and anxieties with Jesus, just as the disciples did on their journey to Emmaus. Although he still needs to develop his affective awareness of God, Steve's capacity to listen to God has improved considerably.

Sister Anne has noticed some changes in the past few months—Steve hinted that he wants to come for spiritual direction more frequently. He calls several times a month just to chat and to see how Anne is doing. He seeks her out at parish activities. In spiritual direction the conversation moves frequently to how appreciative he is to have her in his life. He loves his wife dearly, but he says things such as: "You are the first woman who has really listened to me with such interest and care" or "I'd love to get to know you more, how you feel about things."

Sister Anne is having strong reactions to his attentiveness and needs to process these reactions in supervision.

Questions for Reflection and Discussion after Role-Playing a Supervision Session

1. What stands out to you about the director and the director's experience?

2. What were the director's *reactions* and *reasons* underlying the reactions? What were the *results* of getting in touch with her reactions and reasons?

3. What do you notice about the supervisor and the supervision session? What supervision skills were most operative?

4. How do you feel? What would you help the director explore?

5. What insights about supervision did you gain or have reinforced through this role-playing session?

Case Study 2: Shaun's Experience

Shaun, a fifty-three-year-old executive for a large company, offers spiritual direction at a retreat house on a part-time basis. Married, with four grown children, he has been involved in spiritual direction for more than five years and has a deep love for the ministry. He hopes to become a full-time spiritual director when he retires.

Philip, a social worker in his thirties, has been coming to Shaun for spiritual direction for about six months. He is a very prayerful person who runs a center for homeless people who are addicted to drugs and alcohol. He cares deeply for his clients and is very dedicated to his work.

Shaun and Philip have a very good working relationship as director and directee—Philip feels accepted and safe with Shaun. Shaun has a deep admiration for Philip and his work. Both Philip's prayer and caring ministry have been an inspiration to Shaun. Near the end of the six months, Philip reveals that he is gay. Having worked through and accepted his sexual orientation, he shares this fact about himself for two reasons: he is considering moving in with a man whom he loves very much, and he just found out that his former lover has AIDS. These are two important issues he needs to bring to prayer and to talk about in spiritual direction.

Shaun's initial reaction was a mixture of compassion and numbness. He felt a deep concern for Philip as he courageously shared these realities, but he also felt overwhelmed because it was too much information to absorb in one session. As he reflected and journaled about the session afterward, Shaun experienced an intense fear. He asked himself questions: Am I homophobic without realizing it? Am I fearful of dealing with Philip's possible new lifestyle? or of dealing with the loss of Philip's lover through AIDS? As he pondered these issues, his fear intensified. He needs to process his fear in supervision.

Questions for Reflection and Discussion after Role-Playing a Supervision Session

1. What stands out to you about the director and the director's experience?

2. What were the director's *reactions* and *reasons* underlying the reactions? What were the *results* of getting in touch with his reactions and reasons?

3. What do you notice about the supervisor and the supervision session? What supervision skills were most operative?

4. How do you feel? What would you help the director explore?

5. What insights about supervision did you gain or have been reinforced through this session?

Learning Experience 14

Practicing the Various Aspects of Supervision

In their ongoing education, supervisors must practice the process and skills of supervision. This is particularly important during the early years of supervising because various skills apply and nuances come into play through actual experience. Theory is put into practice in concrete ways. The following group exercise suggests a way to practice and reflect on the various aspects of supervision. They can be used by both spiritual directors being supervised and those doing supervision. At least three people and an hour-and-one-half time period are needed for this learning experience.

Phase 1: A Spiritual Direction Session

Two people conduct a ten- to twelve-minute spiritual direction session. During the session one person shares a real experience of God or life that he or she feels moved to share. The other person takes the stance of a spiritual director. Everyone present is encouraged to enter into a contemplative, God-centered space.

After the session the group spends five to ten minutes of prayerful reflection, keeping the following questions in mind. Then they share their responses with one another.

1. What was noticeable to you about the directee's experience? How would you describe God's presence in this experience?

2. What was striking to you about the director and the spiritual direction session?

3. How did you feel during the session? What did you feel attracted to in the directee's experience? How might you help the person contemplate this?

4. What insights did you gain or were reaffirmed about spiritual direction from this conversation?

Part 2: A Supervision Session

Take fifteen minutes to conduct a supervision session. A third person would supervise the spiritual director who just offered the direction session. The supervisor focuses on the director's interior space, keeping in mind such questions as: What happened in you as you directed this person? How did you feel? What was your strongest feeling? Do you know what was underneath that feeling? The supervisor asks questions, underscores, and uses appropriate supervision skills.

After the session the group takes five to ten minutes of prayerful reflection with the following questions in mind. Then they share their observations with one another.

1. What was noticeable to you about the director's experience? What were the strongest feelings and significant issues that emerged? Where was God in the experience?

2. What stood out to you about the supervisor and the supervision session? What supervision skills mostly applied?

3. How did you feel during the session? What aspect of the experience would you help the director to explore? How would you have done this? What skills would you have used?

4. What insights did you gain or were reaffirmed about supervision?

4. What insight did you gain or were confirmed about relationships?

Learning Experience 15

A Four-Week Supervision Seminar

A valuable way for both spiritual directors and supervisors to learn the various dimensions of supervision is to gather together to discuss, pray, practice, and reflect on the purposes, process, and skills of individual and peer group supervision. Below is a suggested way to conduct a four-week supervision seminar, using the chapters and learning experiences in this book. Each group meeting should be two-and-one-half to three hours in duration, with a facilitator for each gathering to keep time and facilitate the various parts of the class. Each meeting could begin and/or close with a contemplative moment or prayer at the end of one of the chapters being discussed.

Week 1: The Assumptions, Purposes, and Content of Supervision

Preparation

Read chapters 1 and 2. Be prepared to discuss the questions at the end of each chapter. Reflect on learning experiences 1–4.

Group Meeting

1. Discuss each of the chapters and reflection questions.

2. Do a guided meditation based on the prayer experience in learning experience 2 or 4.

3. Conduct a practice session using either one of the case studies in learning experience 13 or the sessions described in learning experience 14.

4. Journal about significant insights learned, either at the end of the class or during the week.

Week 2: The Process and Skills of Supervision

Preparation

Read chapters 3, 4, and 5. Be prepared to discuss the questions at the end of each chapter. Reflect on learning experiences 5 and 6.

Group Meeting

1. Discuss each of the chapters and reflection questions.

2. Role-play one or more of the case studies in chapter 5 and/or learning experience 6 by reading aloud and continuing the conversation.

Share your observations and reflections after each role-play.

3. Conduct a practice session using either one of the case studies in learning experience 13 or the sessions described in learning experience 14.

4. Journal about significant insights learned, either at the end of the class or during the week.

Week 3: Peer Group Supervision

Preparation

Read chapters 6 and 7. Be prepared to discuss the questions at the end of each chapter. Reflect on learning experience 12.

Group Meeting

1. Discuss each of the chapters and reflection questions.

2. Role-play the spiritual direction session and peer group supervision session in chapter 7 by reading aloud and continuing the conversation.

   Share your observations and reflections after the role-play.

3. In groups of four, conduct an actual peer group session using model 1. The presenting director could describe orally the direction situation to be processed.

4. Journal about significant insights learned, either at the end of the class or during the week.

Week 4: Developing a Discerning and Contemplative Heart

Preparation

Read chapters 8, 9, and 10. Be prepared to discuss the reflection questions at the end of each chapter. Reflect on learning experiences 7–11.

Group Meeting

1. Discuss each of the chapters and reflection questions.

2. Do a guided meditation based on the prayer experience in learning experience 9.

3. Prayerfully reflect on and discuss these questions: specifically and concretely, how are you developing a discerning heart as a spiritual director? as a supervisor? How are you developing a contemplative heart?

   Use learning experiences 10 and 11 as a context for this reflection, and enter into the discussion as a faith-sharing experience.

4. Journal about significant insights learned, either at the end of the class or during the week.

Learning Experiences 16-21: Developmental Programs for Spiritual Directors

Specific Recommendations for Developmental Programs

Individuals who are educating spiritual directors must have a clear understanding and agreement concerning the approach, dynamics, focus, and atmosphere of supervision. The following are issues for program staffs to consider.

I. A Common Approach

To avoid confusion, a common approach to individual and peer group supervision among the staff of a training program is necessary. Therefore, a staff needs to spend time together reflecting on the guiding principles undergirding their supervision approach and process as well as other aspects of the program. Learning experiences 17–19 provide reflection questions for staffs of training programs.

II. Individual and Peer Group Supervision

Both individual and peer group supervision are part of a developmental program. Individual supervision allows for in-depth exploration while peer group supervision facilitates a breadth of experiential learnings.

I recommend that the frequency of individual supervision be weekly for a yearlong program and every other week for a two- or three-year program. Peer group supervision should be at least once a month.

III. Verbatim Case Study

A program staff needs to select the specific instrument that will be used during supervision sessions. The two-column verbatim case study of a direction session is ordinarily used in supervision so that spiritual directors can learn from their concrete experiences. However, a process paper or overall case study may be used periodically.

IV. The Focus of Supervision

Although the focus of supervision is on the spiritual director's experience, rather than the directee's experience, the focus can easily shift to the latter. Therefore, supervisors and spiritual directors need to evaluate their supervision sessions to ensure that the primary focus remains on the spiritual director's inner experience. Learning experiences 10 and 11 can facilitate this evaluation.

V. Experienced Spiritual Directors As Supervisors

Supervisors must have at least three year's experience offering spiritual direction and, if possible, have some training in supervision skills for spiritual directors. Workshops and courses on supervision of spiritual directors are now being offered in various parts of the world.

VI. Supervision Seminar

A supervision seminar or a workshop on supervision can be an important learning experience. In addition to providing the means for assimilating the purposes, content, process, and skills, group learning enables everyone in the program to have a common understanding and approach to supervision. Learning experience 15 outlines a four-week supervision seminar.

VII. Supervisors Participating in Supervision

Supervisors need to participate in individual and/or peer group supervision; that is, they need to have their own peer group and/or have a supervisor available.

VIII. Supervisors Evaluating
Supervision Experience Together

Several times in the course of a year it would be advantageous for training program supervisors to evaluate how individual and peer group supervision are progressing. Questions for this reflection can be found in learning experience 19.

IX. Consistent Prayer and Contemplation

To assure that both spiritual direction and supervision are conducted in a contemplative way, a contemplative attitude must permeate all aspects of learning. Such an attitude can be fostered by individual prayer and group prayer experiences, directed retreats for the intern directors, and set times for faith-sharing among directors and supervisors.

Learning Experience 17

Staff Reflection on Guiding Principles

Appendix 1 outlines guiding principles for educating spiritual directors. The following questions can assist a mentoring program staff in reflecting on the total content of their program.

1. What are the guiding principles that govern your program? Do any need to be added?

2. In what ways do your guiding principles reflect those outlined in appendix 1? In what ways are they different?

3. How does your program specifically flesh out each of the key areas—discernment, theological and psychological dimensions, the practicum component, and supervision?

4. What concrete additions or improvements could be made in your program in relation to each of these key areas?

Learning Experience 18

Supervision during a Developmental Program

As the staff of a developmental program reflects on the experience of supervision, the following questions may help.

1. What understanding of the purposes, approach, process, and skills of supervision do you already possess for your program? How are these similar and different from those discussed in this book?

2. What are the attitudes, beliefs, and guiding principles that undergird the approach to supervision for your program?

3. What are you lacking as a group of educators that would sharpen your supervision skills? How can you respond to this need in specific ways?

4. What are the benefits of supervision that each of you have experienced, either by supervising or by being supervised?

5. What model for peer group supervision do you prefer? What are your reasons for choosing this model?

6. How often will your intern spiritual directors have individual supervision? Why? How often will they have peer group supervision? Why?

Staff Evaluation of Supervision Experience

It is helpful for a program staff to meet periodically and reflect together on the supervision experience as it unfolds. The following questions may prove useful.

1. Has your focus in supervision stayed with the spiritual director's experience? If so, what have been the graces, benefits, and insights gleaned from this focus? If not, what has been the focus? How can you move your focus to the director's experience?

2. Has your approach been contemplative and evocative? If so, what graces, benefits, and insights have you gained from this approach? If not, what has been your approach? How can you become more contemplative and evocative?

3. What supervision skills have you found particularly helpful for your intern spiritual directors? For instance, in what ways have you used role-playing during a supervision session? How has role-playing been helpful?

4. How do each of your spiritual directors adjust to and benefit from individual and peer group supervision? In

what specific ways have they grown? What have been some of the challenges?

5. Is there anything that you are doing in supervision that has not been helpful or growth producing for the spiritual directors? What can you do about this?

Learning Experience 20

Directee's Evaluation of Spiritual Direction

In many educational programs, spiritual directors are encouraged initially to meet with their directees more frequently to establish a working relationship between the director and directee, to introduce the process of spiritual direction in a concentrated way, and to ascertain that directees are clear about the focus and purposes of spiritual direction. In some programs, for example, spiritual directors initially meet with their directees weekly for the first eight weeks and then conduct a mutual evaluation with them.

The following questions can facilitate periodic evaluation and reflection on the spiritual direction experience. The results of this reflection can be processed in supervision. Directors then can explore their approach, their focus, their style of spiritual direction, and their strengths and weaknesses.

Directee's Evaluation

1. What do you like about spiritual direction? How have you benefited from it so far?

2. In what specific ways have the sessions themselves been helpful?

3. Has there been anything that was not helpful? something that has been frustrating or counterproductive?

4. Would anything in particular improve the sessions? Are there aspects of the spiritual direction process that remain unclear?

5. What are your desires in seeking spiritual direction? Are they being fulfilled?

6. Specifically, how has spiritual direction helped your prayer life? fostered growth in your relationship with God? your awareness of God's presence in your life circumstances?

Questions for Reflection and Discussion

For Supervisors

1. Do you ask the spiritual directors that you supervise to have a periodic evaluation with their directees and then follow up on these evaluations?

2. Do you feel that directee evaluations are important for the growth of the spiritual director? Why or why not?

3. What have been the concrete benefits of your spiritual directors conducting an evaluation with their directees? Has this helped your work with them? How?

For Spiritual Directors

1. How often do you reflect on the experience of spiritual direction with your directees? Is this sufficient?

2. What have been the fruits and benefits of this evaluation for your directees' experience of spiritual direction and the spiritual direction sessions themselves?

3. What have been the graces and blessings for yourself as a spiritual director? In other words, what have you learned about yourself as a director?

Learning Experience 21

Evaluation Instruments for Spiritual Directors

Educational programs for spiritual directors usually evaluate the participating spiritual directors (associates or interns) once or twice a year. This evaluation can take place in one of three ways:

1. Spiritual directors write a self-evaluation that is read by the program staff. They then meet individually with several of the staff to discuss their growth as spiritual directors.

2. The supervisor of each spiritual director prepares a written evaluation of the director's progress and then discusses it with him or her.

3. Both the supervisor and the spiritual director prepare a written evaluation and discuss it together.

Learning experience 21 describes four evaluation instruments with areas of focus. Instruments 1–3 are prepared by the intern spiritual director for reflection and evaluation with one or more supervisors. Instrument 4 is written by the supervisor and discussed with the spiritual director.

Instrument 1: Personal Progress Report

Directions for Spiritual Director

Prepare a three- to four-page report on your own growth during a particular period. You and your supervisor can determine the two or three areas from the six areas that follow. Explore your growth as well as your growing edges.

In considering these areas, be concrete. Use excerpts from verbatims or from your spiritual direction log to demonstrate your growth. If you are presenting a weak area, be sure to explain the source of this weakness. In sharing an area of growth, mention why you see it as growth and how the growth developed.

Areas for Evaluation

A. **Contemplative Approach to Spiritual Direction**

 1. In what specific ways has your capacity for noticing and savoring your directees' experience of God developed?

 2. How aware are you of the directee's ability to respond to God's touch? How consistent are you in encouraging the directee to respond?

 3. How has your heart and inner space grown more contemplative during direction sessions?

 4. In what ways has your approach and the atmosphere been contemplative and evocative during direction sessions?

B. **Interrelationship between Life and Religious Experience**

 1. Your understanding of this relationship

      a) In what ways has your understanding of the interrelationship between life and religious experience grown? How do you see the relationship?

      b) How does your perception of the interrelationship concretely affect your approach to spiritual direction?

  2. Specific guidelines

      a) In what ways have specific guidelines helped you to determine how long to stay with life experience?

      b) How have they helped you know when to focus on religious experience?

C. Discernment of Movements in Directees

  1. Sifting out interior movements

      a) In what ways has your awareness of various movements (impulses, feelings, images) that lead toward or away from God grown?

      b) When have you noticed these movements in the directee?

      c) How did your awareness of interior movements affect your focus and approach in spiritual direction?

  2. Interior movements within the directee

      a) Describe two movements toward God and two movements away from God that you have noticed in several of your directees.

      b) In what specific ways have you helped directees work through resistance? Use examples from verbatims.

c) What specific guidelines have you found helpful when dealing with resistance in the concrete moment?

d) If you use the *Spiritual Exercises* in a training program, what connections do you see between these movements toward and away from God and the dynamics of the Rules for Discernment?

D. **Discernment of Movements in Yourself as Spiritual Director**

1. Awareness of your interior movements

    a) What has helped you to become aware of interior movements within yourself as you companion others?

    b) Describe two or three countermovements within yourself that can block your freedom to stay with directees' experiences of God.

    c) What issues underlie these countermovements? In what ways are you working with these issues? How have you grown in freedom in relation to these issues?

2. Staying with interior movements

    a) Describe two instances in which you became aware of an area of resistance within yourself. How did you handle it?

    b) State the specific guidelines that you have developed for yourself to deal with your areas of resistance so that they do not infringe on staying with your directees' experiences.

E. **Areas of Strength, Weakness, and Vulnerability**

1. In addition to the areas you already mentioned, are there any other areas of strength or weakness that

would be helpful for you as a spiritual director to explore at this time? Identify each area and the ways you have grown or hope to grow.

2. Are there any personal areas of vulnerability and/or unresolved issues that have become clearer through supervision but still need attention? Specifically, how are you attending to these areas?

F. Your Call As a Spiritual Director

1. In what specific ways has your call as a spiritual director become clearer during this period?

2. Are there any images, or direction sessions, or prayer experiences that have strengthened or confirmed your call?

Instrument 2: Self-Evaluation and Learnings Report

Part I: Self-Evaluation

Directions for Spiritual Director

For this self-evaluation you will use several sources: your experience of being supervised, your supervisor's written and verbal comments, your directees' evaluations and comments, and your knowledge of yourself as a spiritual director.

Prayerfully reflect on these sources. Then write a two-page self-evaluation that includes the following:

1. Areas of strength and affirmation

2. Areas where you need growth—your growing edges

3. Hopes and desires for yourself as a spiritual director

Part II: Personal Learnings

Directions for Spiritual Director

Write a two-page paper on the following areas. From your experience of directing during a particular time frame, what have you concretely learned about

1. God

2. Yourself as a spiritual director and as a person

3. People in spiritual direction

Part III: Progress Report on One Directee

Directions for Spiritual Director

In a two-page paper trace the development or lack of development of one of your directees. Be concrete, giving examples and conversation excerpts.

1. Where was the person with God when he or she began spiritual direction?

2. What shifts have occurred within the person since then? How did you address the shifts?

3. What are the patterns of movement and countermovement?

4. Where does the person seem to be with God now?

5. How are you feeling about the spiritual direction relationship and process with this person?

6. Are there any changes you would like to make in your way of companioning this person?

Instrument 3: Process Paper

Spiritual directors can use this evaluation instrument as a way to synthesize significant insights and graces upon their completion of a two- or three-year program. It also serves as a bridge to the future in that it invites spiritual directors to state concretely the ways that they hope to continue their growth as spiritual directors.

Directions for Spiritual Directors

A. Prayerful reflection on program

Prayerfully reflect on your experience in this program. Write a process paper in which you share some specific reflections, including the following three areas:

1. Ways you have grown as a person and as a spiritual director

2. Growing edges—some specific areas that need growth

3. Several significant graces of the program

B. Commitments after the program

On a separate sheet of paper, state at least two concrete commitments you plan to make for your ongoing growth as a spiritual director and the reasons for these commitments.

Instrument 4: Supervisor's Evaluation

The evaluation instrument is completed by a spiritual director's supervisor at the end of the year. The spiritual director also may prepare a written evaluation using the same instrument. In this way the supervisor and the director would have an evaluation session together in which they share their perceptions of the director's growth.

A. **Supervision Sessions and Supervisory Relationship**

  1. Comment on the spiritual director's preparation for the supervision sessions.

  2. Comment on the director's responsibility in carrying out the supervision contract (for example, preparations of verbatims).

  3. In what ways did the director demonstrate openness and receptivity to your supervision of his or her experiences of directing?

B. **Evaluation of the Spiritual Director's Work**

  1. How does the director prepare personally for direction sessions? Do you think the preparation was adequate and appropriate?

  2. To what extent is the director able to be a companion to directees? In other words, is the director able to stay with directees' content, feelings, and prayer experiences?

  3. How is the director's ability to assist directees in recognizing and exploring areas of struggle, personal weakness, and/or sinfulness?

  4. In what ways did the director deal with the patterns of consolation and desolation in directees?

  5. In which areas did the spiritual director, through experience and reflection, develop spiritual direction and discernment skills?

  6. In which areas does the director need more growth as a spiritual director? as a person?

C. Recommendations

1. What would you recommend to this spiritual director for further professional growth?

2. What would you recommend to this director for further personal growth? for continued attention to vulnerable areas and unresolved issues?

Questions for Reflection and Discussion for a Program Staff

1. What are the advantages and disadvantages of each of the four evaluation instruments?

2. Which evaluation instrument would be most appropriate for your program? Why?

3. Which evaluation instrument would be used more beneficially at mid-year evaluation? at year-end evaluation?

4. What other evaluation instruments can be used besides the four described in this chapter?

Appendix 1:
Guiding Principles
for Developmental Programs

A growing number of training programs for spiritual directors are being developed throughout the world. Because of the quantity and diversity of programs, a symposium for educators and supervisors of spiritual directors was organized in 1989 and has met each year since then. The question of licensing spiritual directors has been discussed frequently with a variety of views. The participants at the symposium also have considered the possibility of certifying programs, thus assuring that all of them have similar components and guiding principles. At the 1991 symposium in Chestnut Hill, Pennsylvania, the participants prepared a tentative list of guiding principles for educators of spiritual directors to consider in formulating and evaluating their programs. These principles are still under discussion. The following is a list of the tentative principles concerning five key areas that emerged from this symposium.

Discernment
Theological Dimensions
Psychological Dimensions
Practicum
Supervision

A. Discernment

- Call

- Competency

- Ongoing process

- Communal discernment

- Context in which discernment occurs historical/ social/economic/cultural

- Spiritual dimensions—Contemplative attitude

B. Theological dimensions

- Traditions

- Single tradition

- Operational assumptions of the Christian tradition

- Contemplative attitude

- Spirituality—prayer dimension

- Religious experience

  The word *pluralistic* needs to be added to our concept of religious experiences—we must be open to ideas that are perhaps not fully Christian yet are developing a strong interest.

- The New Age phenomenon needs to be addressed.

- Anthropology

- Awareness of popular movements

- Scripture and tradition

- A Gospel-centered spirituality and Christology

C. Psychological dimensions

- Reflection on life experience

- Awareness of popular movements (Enneagram/ Myers-Briggs)

- Healthy self-knowledge and self-acceptance

- Anthropological assumptions

- Dysfunctions

- Exposure to depth and developmental psychology

- Various models that honor male and female

- Healthy awareness of boundaries

D. Practicum

- Supervised direction as central tool

- Real play instead of role-playing

- Some form of integration

- Responsibility to directees and student directors

- Confidentiality

- A contemplative approach and attitude

E. Supervision

- Focus on spiritual director's inner experience

- Individual supervision and peer group supervision

- Common approach by staff

- Training of supervisors

- Supervisors' participation in supervision

- Consultation

Appendix 2:
Ongoing Associate Program for the Development of Spiritual Directors

While presenting workshops, programs, courses, and retreats in various parts of the country, I have had the privilege of meeting many spiritual directors with hopes of establishing a developmental program in their area. They ask questions: What is involved in the education of spiritual directors? What are the components? What kind of background should people have who are interested in becoming spiritual directors? How do people know when they are being called to the ministry? How often do participants meet? How long is a program? What does it cost to participate?

Although many programs are moving toward a uniform focus and list of guiding principles (as outlined in appendix 1), the answers to these questions vary, depending on the length of the program, the number of staff members, and the number of people accepted into the program.

Appendix 2 and appendix 3 describe two developmental programs at the Upper Room Spiritual Center in Neptune, New Jersey. The first description, a three-year, part-time program in existence since 1982, stresses ongoing (monthly) spiritual direction. The second, a two- to three-year part-time program established in 1986, emphasizes directed-retreat spiritual direction.

Ongoing Associate Program
for the Development of Spiritual Directors

I. Purpose

The associate program for ongoing spiritual direction is a part-time, three-year program. Its purpose is

A. to discern with associates their gifts and a call to do spiritual direction;

B. to develop their gifts and to facilitate their response;

C. to prepare associates to serve in the ministry of spiritual direction in a specific parish and/or recognized community of faith; and

D. to respond to the need and desire of those who wish to receive spiritual direction from someone prepared for this ministry.

II. Approach to spiritual direction

A. Assumptions

1. God desires to relate to persons as individuals and as a community.

2. This relationship grows through prayer and in life experience.

3. Dialogue with a spiritual director is significant for growing awareness of and response to one's experience of God.

4. Directors' own prayer and personal growth have an integral relationship to the way they companion others in spiritual direction.

B. Common approach

The team at the center has developed a common approach to spiritual direction and an agreement: hours of individual supervision and theological studies; number of directees; peer group supervision; and theological reflection.

Summary of the approach is as follows:

Spiritual direction facilitates growth in a loving relationship between a person and God through focusing on mutual self-disclosure and self-giving. It enables one to notice, stay with, and respond to God's presence in life and prayer, and to grow in an even more intimate relationship with God. The focus of spiritual direction is religious experience, that is, how God communicates to an individual and how that person responds to God's self-communication in one's inner and outer life.

III. Elements of the associate program

A. Experience of receiving and offering spiritual direction

1. Receiving spiritual direction

a) Ongoing spiritual direction

During the program associates continue to receive spiritual direction regularly.

b) Two directed retreats are held each year during the first two years.

(1) Associates are directed by their supervisors during a retreat in September and in January of each year.

(2) Reasons for retreats:

(a) to help supervisors gain greater knowledge of the associates' prayer life; and

(b) to provide an opportunity for bonding between associates and supervisors.

2. Offering spiritual direction

a) Number of directees (by the end of each year)

(1) First-year associates: six directees

(2) Second-year associates: twelve directees

(3) Third-year associates: sixteen directees

b) Practical aspects of directing

(1) Through an intake interview the team confirms a person's desire and readiness to receive spiritual direction.

(2) The director and directee establish a "contract" and clarify the nature of the spiritual direction relationship.

(3) An evaluation based on this contract takes place at the end of eight weeks.

(4) At least one directee continues on a weekly basis after the evaluation.

c) Reasons for weekly direction/frequent direction:

(1) to facilitate the associate to notice movements more;

(2) to assist the directee in learning to pray in a personal way;

(3) to help the directee to clarify and stay with his or her experience of God when a great deal is happening in prayer;

(4) to aid a directee in paying attention to God, especially in a crisis situation; and

(5) to provide an opportunity for trust to grow between the director and the directee.

3. Intake interviews

a) An intake interview takes place with individuals who desire to receive spiritual direction.

b) First-year associates learn how to conduct intake interviews.

B. Individual and group supervision

1. Individual supervision

The key to learning the dynamics, process, and skills of spiritual direction is through supervision. The overall purpose of supervision is to help spiritual directors grow in self-awareness and interior freedom in order to stay with directees' experiences and be attentive to God during direction sessions. This overall purpose has several dimensions.

a) Discerning movements in oneself as a spiritual director:

(1) to sift interior movements leading toward and away from God; and

(2) to recognize experiential reasons for countermovements.

b) Becoming aware of resistance and emotional blocks:

(1) to grow in greater awareness of areas of resistance that could prevent the director from delving deeper into another's experience; and

(2) to explore past and present experiences and issues that affect the spiritual direction relationship.

c) Growth in interior freedom to linger with directees' experiences.

2. Peer group supervision once a month

C. Theological reflection

1. Courses, professional days, and workshops

Various courses and workshops are offered on growth in prayer, the experience of God, spiritual direction, supervision, discernment, the *Spiritual Exercises,* group spiritual direction, psychological and theological issues, and other matters involving spiritual direction.

2. Required readings and reading discussion sessions

Sessions feature different themes for each of the three years.

3. Evaluations

   a) Mid-year and end-of-year evaluations are conducted during first two years with the program staff. In general the purposes of these evaluations are twofold:

      (1) to facilitate the continual discernment of the associate's call to the ministry of spiritual direction; and

      (2) to evaluate the progress and growth of associate spiritual directors.

   b) Process paper during third year

      Third-year associates write a process paper as an opportunity to reflect on their experience and to gather the graces.

4. Weekend of prayer and discernment (end of year):

   a) to pray over the experience of directing during the year in relation to one's call, blessings, inadequacies, strengths, and desires for the future;

   b) to faith-share on these themes with the other associate spiritual directors; and

   c) to deepen bonds of caring and sharing among associates.

IV. Program staff

The program staff has had formal training in spiritual direction and individually directed retreats, extensive theological education, and years of experience in the ministry of spiritual direction. (The names and educational background of each person would be stated here.)

V. Application information and procedures

   A. Personal prerequisites

      1. Two years of ongoing spiritual direction on a one-to-one and regular basis (at least monthly)

      2. B.A. or B.S. degree

      3. Sufficient knowledge in the areas of theology, Scripture, psychology, and spirituality

      4. Psychological, spiritual, and personal maturity

      5. At least thirty-three years old

      6. A thirty-day directed retreat or an individualized and full-year Nineteenth Annotation Retreat based on the *Spiritual Exercises*

   B. Sponsoring body

      1. Philosophy

It is our firm conviction that the ministry of spiritual direction is rooted in the history and the life of the Church. Further, we believe that it is grounded in and supported by a community of faith. Therefore, as we discern about those accepted as associates, we consider it essential that each applicant have a sponsoring body who supports the associate personally, spiritually, and financially (associates may also help with finances).

      2. Description

        a) A parish

        b) A religious congregation

        c) A diocese

       d) A spiritual center or retreat house

    3. Commitment from sponsoring body

       When an individual begins the formal application process, a contract will be signed by the leader of the faith community. Several elements are included.

       a) Agreement about length of time associate will spend in the program as well as a room to do spiritual direction

       b) Agreement about having the associate serve as a spiritual director after the program is completed

       c) Agreement about financial arrangements

C. Application process

    1. Initial application includes

       a) a typed letter of intent containing the following:

          (1) biographical data (including educational and theological background);

          (2) reasons for applying and desires concerning the ministry of spiritual direction; and

          (3) information about one's own spiritual direction, that is, frequency, duration, and style of direction.

       b) A letter from the sponsoring body

    2. Application form and interview

       a) An extensive application form is sent.

        b)   Staff interviews each applicant.

D.   Time involvement

   1.   First and second year

        a)   Associates initially direct two people on a weekly basis (one hour each session). The number of directees is increased during the program.

        b)   Individual supervision—every other week

           (1) A verbatim is prepared for each supervision session. A verbatim is a typed conversation that includes background and reflections and represents a significant experience and exchange in the direction session.

           (2) Supervision extends from September to late May

        c)   Peer group supervision—eight times a year

        d)   Required readings and reading discussion sessions

        e)   Required courses (topics vary each year)

        f)   Professional days for spiritual directors (topics vary each year)

        g)   Two directed retreats

        Each September and January, associates make a three-day directed retreat with their supervisors as their directors.

        h)   Prayer and discernment weekend in April

   i)   Mid-year and final evaluations

  2.   Third year

   a)   Associates direct twelve to sixteen people

   b)   Four individual supervision sessions and eight peer group supervision sessions

   c)   Required readings and reading discussion sessions

   d)   Required courses, including "How to Give the Nineteenth Annotation Retreat"

   e)   Professional days for spiritual directors

   f)   Two directed retreats under supervision

    (1)   Associates bring three retreatants

    (2)   Purpose: Provides an opportunity for spiritual direction in a more intensified setting

   g)   Prayer and discernment weekend in April

   h)   Final process paper and meeting with a supervisor

 E. Finances

  1.   Application fee

  2.   Annual tuition

  3.   Retreat fees and other costs

Appendix 3:
Retreat Associate Program
for the Development
of Spiritual Directors

What (Description)

The Retreat Associate Program for the Development of Spiritual Directors is an opportunity for experienced spiritual directors to deepen their personal and professional growth. Offered in the context of directed retreats, the program has three components: (1) giving directed prayer weekends and longer directed retreats, (2) experiencing daily supervision during these retreats, and (3) engaging in a series of readings related to directed retreats, spiritual direction, and the *Spiritual Exercises*.

Why (Objectives)

1. To refine spiritual direction skills in the more concentrated atmosphere of directed retreats

2. To receive supervision in order to deepen one's self-awareness and further one's growth as a spiritual director

3. To provide an opportunity for those whose primary training and experience has been in ongoing spiritual direction to broaden their development as spiritual directors

4. To experience the support of other spiritual directors
through ministering and learning with others

5. To deepen one's knowledge and understanding of religious experience, spiritual direction, and directed retreats

Who (Participants)

1. Individuals who have received certification in spiritual
direction from a program that focuses primarily on ongoing spiritual direction; and/or

2. Individuals who have experience in giving ongoing spiritual direction and/or directed retreats

How (Structure)

1. Thirty days of directing retreats according to the following structure:

   a) Nine directed prayer weekends (total: eighteen days)

   b) Two six-day directed retreats (total: twelve days)

2. Directees—two or three people for each retreat

   a) Directors bring two or three people.

   b) The Upper Room provides directees when needed.

3. Supervision

   a) Directors receive individual supervision each day
   during all the retreats.

b) During longer retreats daily peer group supervision sessions will be offered and required readings assigned.

c) Supervision will be conducted according to individual needs and experience.

d) During the duration of the program, participants receive supervision from at least two supervisors.

4. Readings

 a) Articles and books

 b) Debriefing readings with supervisors

When (Time Frame)

1. The program is usually completed within two years. However, some individuals may choose to finish in three years.

2. The Upper Room schedules monthly directed prayer weekends each year. Directors can arrange with the program administrator the desired dates.

3. A six-day directed retreat is offered each spring and summer (usually May and August).

4. Certification: Upon fulfillment of the program, participants receive a Certificate of Completion.

Finances

1. Tuition

2. Retreat and supervision fees

3. Total cost of program

Application Procedures

1. For further information contact the program coordinator.

2. If interested in applying to the program, send an application letter to the program coordinator, including

    a) autobiographical details (education and ministerial experience, certification, and/or experience in giving spiritual direction) and

    b) reasons and desires for participating in the program

Suggested Reading

Spiritual Direction

Barry, William, and William J. Connolly. *The Practice of Spiritual Direction*. New York: Seabury Press, 1982.

Birmingham, Madeline, and William J. Connolly. *Witnessing to the Fire: Spiritual Direction and the Development of Directors*. Kansas City, Mo.: Sheed and Ward, 1994.

Conroy, Maureen, R.S.M. *The Discerning Heart: Discovering a Personal God*. Chicago: Loyola University Press, 1993.

————. *Growing in Love and Freedom: Personal Experiences of Counseling and Spiritual Direction*. Denville, N.J.: Dimension, 1987.

Fischer, Kathleen. *Women at the Well: Feminist Perspectives on Spiritual Direction*. Mahwah, N.J.: Paulist Press, 1988.

Ganss, George E. *The Spiritual Exercises of Saint Ignatius: A Translation and Commentary*. St. Louis, Mo.: Institute of Jesuit Sources, 1992.

Kelsey, Morton T. *Companions on the Inner Way: The Art of Spiritual Guidance*. New York: Crossroad, 1989.

May, Gerald G., M.D. *Care of Spirit/Care of Mind: Psychiatric Dimensions of Spiritual Direction*. San Francisco: Harper and Row, 1982.

Ruffing, Janet. *Uncovering Stories of Faith: Spiritual Direction and Narrative*. Mahwah, N.J.: Paulist Press, 1989.

Supervision

Barry, William A. "Supervision Improves Ministry." *Human Development* 9, no. 1 (spring 1988): 27–30.

Estadt, Barry, John Compton, and Melvin Blanchette, eds. *The Art of Clinical Supervision: A Pastoral Counseling Perspective*. Mahwah, N.J.: Paulist Press, 1987.

Index